OSHUN
PUBLISHING CO., INC.

10 9 8 7 6 5 4 3 2 1

Oshun Publishing Company, Inc.
7717 Crittenden Street
Suite 377
Philadelphia, PA   19118

**Book design and illustration by
Marion Designs**

ISBN 0-9676028-2-3

Printed in Canada

The Guide to Becoming the Sensuous Black Woman (And Drive Your Man Wild In and Out Of Bed!)

by
"Miss T."

visit *The Guide To Becoming the Sensuous Black Woman* website at www.*sensuousblackwoman.com*

This Book is Dedicated to all My

Beautiful Black Sistas

Table of Contents

Contents

Introduction

About Me – And Why I Decided To Write This Book

Who am I? Well, I personally don't believe who I am, or who wrote this book, is important as long as it's been written. I believe a book such as this is long past due. But my dear publisher insists that I say a little something something about myself.

This is particularly hard to do since I prefer to remain anonymous -- hence my decision to use the pseudonym "Miss T." But since I agreed to write a little about myself, I shall.

I was raised in both New York City and Washington D.C. and am in my early forties (You don't really believe I should reveal my exact age, do you?) and of course I'm a working girl. No! Not that kind of working girl. Ladies, please . . . get your minds out of the gutter!

I grew up believing I wasn't pretty and since I so convinced myself, other people just naturally followed my cue. I find it hard to believe now, but I -- like so many women -- suffered from very low-esteem. I was therefore willing to do anything to get and keep a man, and then couldn't understand why no man really wanted me for long.

It wasn't until I was almost twenty that I realized how ridiculous I was being, and how cruel I had been to myself. I then took it upon myself to study the women around me whom I admired to find out what it was about them that made them so different from me. The first thing I noticed was their attitude. They had this air about them that said "I've got it going on, and any man should be proud to have me on his arm. But I'm not giving myself to just any man."

Then I had to study further to figure out what the hell it was they had going on.

I was a good student, and I learned quickly and thoroughly -- and now I've decided to pass the information on.

For years, friends and colleagues have come to me asking me for advice about men because they've seen my success with the opposite sex. I've always tried to help, but really only in dribs and drabs. I never sat anyone down to give any of them a full blow-by-blow exposition. Not because I was being selfish, but because I was being lazy.

A few years ago I was having lunch with an old friend, Karen E. Quinones Miller, and I jokingly said that I should write a how-to book on getting a man, and while we were eating we kind of fleshed out the idea and came to agreement about what should be in the book. It went from a 'how-to book on getting a man' to a 'how-to book on a woman meeting her potential of becoming a fully sensuous woman.' And that's how "The Guide To Becoming A Sensuous Black Woman, (And Drive Your Man Wild In And Out Of Bed!)" came to be. Of course it still took me about five years to get around to writing the book, but it's finally finished, and I hope you'll get a lot out of it. It was important to me that this book not just be a sex manual, but a guide for women to discover their sensuality, and realize what wonderful beings we all are. I think I've accomplished my goal.

But ladies, I really do hope we can keep these secrets to ourselves. Oh, I mean I hope you will (I encourage you to) share these secrets with your sistas, but please don't go around spouting them off to the men folks. They don't need to know what we're doing – God knows they don't teach us the little tricks they use on us, but they sure seem ready to pass them from one brotha to another.

So this is all about sistahood, okay? These are all things we need to know and share with each other, but only with each other. Let this be our bond.

All of the information contained in this book should be information that should be taught us while we're young, so we don't go through that awkward stage of trying to figure things out on our own. I even think it would be great if the organizations that host Rites-of-Passage programs for girls would give each a copy of this book.

So why do I want to remain anonymous? Well, some of the material contained in "The Guide To Becoming The Sensuous Black Woman" is rather risqué, but that's okay. It's just that I'm not willing to publicly take on the mantle of sex-expert and I know that's how a lot of people will see me after reading this book. Let me also state that I don't think there's anything wrong with the mantle, but it would upset my life right now, and right now I don't want my life upset. I hope you can understand.

For that reason I'm going to be on the down-low, at least for the moment.

For those who don't know, I have a website up (well, my editor put it up for me) so please stop by at www.sensuousblackowman.com and let me know what you think of the book.

So I hope you enjoy my book, but more importantly, I hope you get a lot out of it. People are already bugging me to write another book, and maybe I'll break down and do just that. So keep posted!

What is a Sensuous Black Woman?

Am I beautiful? No? My nose is a little bit too small. My lips are a little too thin. My butt is a little too narrow. But when I walk into a room I'm often thought to be stunning. I'm the woman who men take one look at and start drooling.

It's not just the way I dress, although, girlfriends, I dress to kill. When I go to work I wear off the rack clothing, bought from Bloomingdale's, Saks Fifth Avenue, and Lord and Taylor. When I go out on the town I wear custom made gowns and jewelry from

Tiffany's. My hair is always fierce, and if I don't feel like doing my make-up myself, I have a licensed cosmetologist come to my home and do it for me. Uh-huh, I dress to kill. But it's not clothes that make this woman.

It's my attitude.

It's the way I carry myself.

It's my sensuality.

My highly tuned sensuality means I'm great at sex (actually I'm fantastic!), but it also means so much more. Sensuality is fully experiencing life through awareness, presence and the exploration of your senses.

When I eat I don't just gobble up my food, I take my time and savor the taste. When I catch a whiff of a fragrance I close my eyes and let it take me away. When I touch, I delight in the texture beneath my fingers. And when I am touched, anywhere on my body, I feel it all the way through to my soul, and I uninhibitedly respond.

People can merely look at me and tell I am in tune with my senses, my sexuality, my desires, my being, and I'm not only comfortable with my senses, I revel in them. I am a sensual being. I am The Sensuous Black Woman.

And it simply drives men wild.

Wild enough that by the time I was twenty-four, two different men had bought me cars for my birthday. By the time I was twenty-seven I had enough diamond jewelry to make Marie Antoinette jealous. By the time I was thirty I had taken trips to ten different foreign countries. Men don't just do this because I'm great in bed, but because they want to spend every waking moment with me. By just allowing them to be with me I satisfy all of their desires, in and out of bed. Do I sound conceited? I'm just being honest. By way of proof of this fact, I've had more marriage proposals than I'll even bother to recount. And not just from the around-the-way guys, but from doctors, lawyers, architects, rap stars, and Wall Street brokers.

Not bad for a girl from the South Bronx, huh?

I'm not the first Sensuous Black Woman. The Queen of Sheba had King Solomon writing songs about her back in Biblical times. Other Sensuous Black Women include Cleopatra (sensual enough to drive both Julius Caesar and Mark Anthony crazy), Josephine Baker (ever seen a picture of her doing the Banana Dance? Ooh la la!), Lena Horne (she can give lessons on how to wear a mink stole with bare shoulders), Eartha Kitt (oh how she purrs!), Aaliyah (she's timeless!), Vanessa Williams (whether you argue she's "black enough" or not, she's still black, and sensual as hell. I claim her!) and Beyonce (it's not just her big booty, it's how she uses it, honey.).

In fact, I'd go so far as to say that no woman has more capacity for sensuality than a black woman. (Did you know that black women are 50 percent more likely to reach orgasm every time they have sex than white women?) It's evidenced by the sensual sway of our hips as we walk, the way music just naturally makes us move, and our natural compassion for people we perceive as less fortunate than ourselves. It's just that sometimes with the crap we have to deal with living in a country that has always put us down we sometimes find it hard to accept ourselves as sensual beings. Can you believe that the Miss America contest went forty-nine years before a black woman was able to compete? And fifty-four years before a black woman actually won the contest?

Which reminds me, this might be a good time to talk about the difference between a Beautiful Black woman and a Sensuous Black Woman. Vanessa Williams, the dethroned 1984 Miss America is sensuous. Suzette Charles, the black woman who ascended to the throne after Miss Williams, was beautiful, but not sensuous. She is pretty as all hell, but just didn't have that "it" thing going for her that makes a woman a Sensuous Black Woman. Halle Berry is probably one of the most beautiful black women in the world, but I can't give it to her as far as sensuality. Both women make men go "ahhh", but they don't have that special thing that would make a man do anything in the world to be with them. They don't have the awareness of themselves, or the very apparent confidence in themselves, to be considered a Sensuous Black Woman.

And I'll also take the time to talk about the difference between sexy and sensuous. You can be sexy but not sensuous, but it's impossible to be sensuous without being sexy. For instance, Lil Kim is sexy as all hell. As one male friend of mine put it, "You know she's a freak in bed. I'd like to take her home and fuck her until she bleeds." Okay, a bit crass, but you catch the drift. Eve, on the other hand, is a sensuous black woman. The type of woman a man wants to escort to an awards celebration, wine and dine her afterward, take her home for a night of alternating fucking and love-making, and then have breakfast with in the morning.

No, it's not just sex that makes a woman sensual.

Back in days of old, French courtesans and Japanese geisha girls were considered the most sexually talented women in the world, but they were so much more than that. They were gracious and graceful, well-read and well-spoken, intelligent and attentive; all necessary qualities of a sensuous woman. The one quality they also possessed that I just can't get with was their subservience, if that can be called a quality. Personally, I speak my mind, although I try not to be rude while doing so. And I've found that most men whom I want to be around, and whom I would allow to be around me, enjoy my outspokenness. Smart men don't want stupid puppets.

Was I always The Sensuous Black Woman? I believe that innately all black women are, but I didn't fully realize my potential until I was nineteen.

I had just broken up with my boyfriend and was sitting in front of the television eating a pint of pistachio ice cream, crying my eyes out between spoonfuls. I had been with James for six months and in the time he'd been through both my savings and checking accounts, stolen my VCR and screwed my best friend. And then after all that, he dumped me!

And I was stupid enough to be worrying about what was wrong with me. What had I done wrong that this man whom I worshipped would leave me?

Was I stupid or what?

One of those "Calgon, take me away" commercials came on, and I put down the empty container of ice cream and went into the bathroom. Damn, if I didn't need something to take me away, you know? I didn't have any Calgon™, but I did have some bath salts someone had given me for Christmas the year before. I dumped the whole bottle in the tub. Would you believe just as I got ready to jump in, the light bulb blew? And of course I didn't have any more light bulbs. So, I dug out some scented votive candles that someone else had given me for another Christmas, lit two, and hopped into the bath. I just lay there, partially submerged in the tub for about five minutes, still sniffling and feeling sorry for myself. Then I started feeling a tingly sensation around my breasts and between my legs. I didn't know it when I had dumped the bath salts in the tub, but they were actually effervescent mineral bath crystals, and they were doing their thing, fizzing and popping and popping and fizzing.

I'd never been one for masturbating, and truth be told what I had called masturbating was simply rubbing my poor clit raw whenever I read a hot section in a sexy book. But that day my hand started doing some wandering.

It started innocently enough. It was warm in the bathroom, and with the heat from the hot water in the tub, my face had begun to lightly perspire. After I wiped my brow I let my hand slowly trail down my cheek, then my throat and then between my breasts. It lingered there for a moment, then, as if my hand had a mind of it's own, I found I was cupping my left breast. My nipples were harder than they'd ever been when I was with James. My fingers twirled around them for a moment, and then my other hand started trailing down my stomach past my navel, and suddenly I found myself gently raking my fingernails through my pubic hair with one hand, while squeezing and softly pinching my nipples with the other. And the strangest thing was that I wasn't fantasizing about anyone or thinking about anything erotic or sexual while I was doing this. I was just feeling good, and allowing myself to make me feel even better.

I finally let my fingers travel further down, and I opened my legs wider and parted the lips to my vagina, and in doing so gave those wonderful effervescent crystals more access to the most sensitive spots on my body. Oh it was heaven! Instead of starting at the top of my clitoris, I moved my fingers to my slit, though I didn't enter my vagina. I moved my fingers up through the crevice of my clitoris so that my hood was fully open. I hesitated for just a moment and took a deep breath, then I simply touched my fully exposed love button (aka clitoris glans) with one finger, and I started cumming. It was like nothing I had ever felt. I didn't have violent spasms, and I wasn't wildly gyrating or screaming or holding back screams, the way I usually do during orgasms. This was different. Almost serene. It was like my body was giving out the most deep, relaxing and enjoyable sigh. Even after it was over, I could still feel that warm sensation.

I lay in the tub for another ten minutes before I finally dragged myself out and dried myself off. I noticed that I was more aware of the fluffiness of the towel than I had ever been before, and I realized it was because I wasn't roughly rubbing myself with the terry cloth, but more so caressing my skin with it. I was pampering myself. And I liked it.

Needless to say I took another bath the next evening, and even though I had already put in a new light bulb, I turned off the light and instead of using two candles I had five. And this time I added music – a mixed tape featuring an assortment of light jazz and love songs. Same result, honey.

The following evening I added rose petals to the water along with the mineral bath crystals, and sipped a glass of champagne while relaxing in the tub. That night I didn't touch myself, but I still got out of the tub feeling warm and sensuous. I walked into the bedroom, naked, and looked at myself in my full-length mirror. For the first time that I could remember in a long while, I looked at myself with admiration rather than a critical eye. What a beautiful woman there was in the reflection smiling back at me. I wondered why I never noticed that before. Why had I always dwelt on my physical shortcomings? I vowed I would never put myself down again, and I would certainly never let any man make me feel bad. To hell with James. He should be worshipping at my feet, I decided. Come to think of it, I thought as I twirled my naked body in the mirror, so should every man.

Right then and there, a sensuous black woman came to be.

It took some studying, some observation, and a lot of trial and error, but it wasn't long before I was driving men wild, in and out of bed.

And as you read my little book you'll see how you can, too.

<u>Preparing Yourself to Become The Sensuous Black Woman</u>

"What can I say, we're fighting again," my cousin told me after I almost collided with her boyfriend as he stomped out of the door of her apartment cursing.

I didn't bother to ask what they were fighting about because my dear cuz had been on the telephone all month telling me how he was staying out late, and that she thought he was having an affair, although she couldn't prove it.

Turns out though, she didn't care that I didn't care. She started spilling her guts almost as soon as I walked in. Which pissed me off because I was supposed to take her to Bloomingdale's to pick out her belated birthday present, but I also had a lunch date at the Plaza that I'd been looking forward to all week. And when my cousin got started talking about her problems, she never knew when to stop.

"I know he's cheating on me, girl, I know he is. And even though I know it I'm not throwing him out. I just refuse to have sex with him unless he wears a condom. I'm not catching a case of the clap because he doesn't know how to keep his johnson in his pants. I don't think that's unreasonable, do you?"

I looked at my watch, but she refused to take the hint.

"I even went out and bought the damn condoms and gave them to him. You'd think he'd be grateful, wouldn't you?" And then, horror of all horrors, my cousin started crying, I mean really bawling. Well, I had to say something.

"Look. I think you have every right to want him to wear a condom, but maybe you're going about it the wrong way," I told her as I tried to calm her down. "Instead of just throwing a bunch of rubbers at him, maybe you can convince him to wear one by putting it on him yourself. Men love that shit."

"I offered to, but he still refuses," she said, wiping her eyes.

"Really? Well, you do know how to put one on, right?" I asked.

"Sure. I mean, it's not rocket science," she said sarcastically.

"Yeah, okay, then show me how you do it."

"What?" she looked up at me in surprise.

"You said you have condoms, right? Show me how you put one on."

"I've got condoms, but uh," she started to giggle, "I don't have a dick."

"Got a cucumber?"

Then I sat there and watched her roughly shove a newly opened condom on the poor unsuspecting cucumber. If I were her boyfriend I wouldn't let her anywhere near my penis. She gave me one of those "What the hell is wrong with you" looks when she heard me groan out loud.

I pulled out my cell phone and reluctantly canceled my date. The things we do for family.

"Look, let me show you how to put on a condom," I said. I opened another condom and put it down on the table, then picked up cucumber. I held it in both hands and kissed the tip, then slowly and gently rubbed it against my cheek.

"Ooh, girl, you're just nasty," my cousin said with a laugh.

I winked at her, then brought the cucumber to my lips and kissed it again, then gave it a slow twirl with my tongue. Then I reached over and picked up the condom and placed it in my mouth, and then slowly rolled it down the cucumber. (Don't worry. You'll learn the technique in Chapter Four.) My cousin gasped. I leaned back in my chair and handed her the now sheathed vegetable. "I bet he wouldn't have any problems wearing a rubber if you put it on him like that," I told her with a grin.

My cousin is a slow learner, so it took about seven condoms before she got the knack of it, and I wound up staying another few hours after that going over other little tips I figured she could use.

Not only did I miss my lunch date at the Plaza, I almost blew my early dinner date at Tavern on the Green. But I figured it was worth it when she called me the next morning gushing with happiness. They went through three condoms the night before, she told me, and not one of them was wasted. She called me again a couple of weeks later to thank me again. Not only was he happily wearing condoms, he wasn't staying out late anymore. Turns out that my teaching her that little technique inspired her to come up with a few more tricks of her own. Seems he was now getting everything he needed right there at home. They've now been married for three years, and because she's secure that they have a monogamous relationship she no longer makes him wear condoms, but sometime they use it just for the hell of it. I take credit for putting my cousin on the path to becoming a Sensuous Black Woman.

And now I want to put you on that same path.

I'm sure you've already looked at the table of contents and seen that my techniques for driving a man wild in bed are in Chapter 4, but I hope you don't decide to jump to that chapter without first reading this chapter and the next, because in order to become The Sensuous Black Woman and get to work on him you have to first work on you! So be patient, and read on.

Tuning Your Confidence
Self-confidence is both sexy and sensuous. There's nothing more thrilling then when a man with an air of "I've got it going on" decides to focus his energy on seducing you, right? Well a man feels the same way about a self-confident woman. It's not so much that he's impressed with her self-confidence as much as

it is that he's impressed that someone so confident finds him worthy of her attention. It's a turn-on!

But self-confidence can't be faked. You've got to know you've got it going on before everyone else will realize you've got it going on. So let's start by:

Getting naked and looking at yourself in the mirror!

Don't go eek. And don't say, "I'm going to skip this step." Be brave ladies!

Okay. What do you see? A little cellulite? Big deal! Don't you know that most women over thirty (and a significant amount of women under thirty) have cellulite? Even supermodels have cellulite, which is why photographers get paid so much to airbrush pictures for magazines. Most men I've spoken to could give less than a hoot about it.

Sagging breasts? Yeah, gravity is a bitch. But that's why God made push-up bras, dearie.

But stop focusing on your so-called flaws, and look what you've got going for you. Maybe it's your eyes. Maybe it's the shape of your lips. Maybe it's the curve of your legs. Maybe it's your tiny waist. Maybe it's your big butt. The thing is you have *something* -- why not spend as much time complimenting and accentuating your good physical qualities as you've spent criticizing and feeling bad about your imperfections? And if focusing on your so-called flaws can make you feel horrible, shouldn't focusing on your assets make you feel great?

And listen, don't think because you're heavy you can't be a Sensuous Black Woman – just ask comedienne Monique. It's so unfortunate that so many of our full-figured sistas suffer from low self-esteem based solely on their weight.

Also, you're never too old to be a Sensuous Black Woman. Tina Turner is sexy even now that she's in her sixties. Eartha Kitt is still a sex kitten in her seventies.

Okay, you can get out of the mirror and put your clothes back on (for now) because next we're going to work on:

Tuning your senses

In order to become a Sensuous Black Woman you have to be in tune with your senses. Why? Because the more in tune you are with your senses the more pleasure you tend to get out of life – and the more pleasure you want to give others. And the better you are at giving pleasure. And people around you can intuitively sense this.

So how do you get in tune with your senses? By exercising them the way you exercise your body to build up your muscles. I'd like for you to try a few exercises – but no more than one exercise a night.

1. <u>Sense of Taste</u>

We all love to eat and enjoy eating tasty food, but how many of you savor the taste? What I'd like you to do is get a small bowl of warm chocolate (the kind you'd use for fondue), turn off the lights and fire up some candles, and get comfortable on your couch. Make sure the television is off, and while you can do this exercise with music, the first time around it's best to do without. I want you to concentrate on only your sense of taste only for now.

Slowly dip your entire index finger in the chocolate and swirl it around, then leisurely bring your finger to your parted lips and flick your tongue out and take a long slow lick. Now close your eyes and savor the taste and texture. Mmm, so sweet. So smooth and creamy. So good you know you want more.

Go ahead, open your eyes and dip again. But this time, instead of one long lick of the finger, do a series of short licks with your tongue, starting from the bottom of your finger. When you get to the tip of your finger, close your eyes and twirl your tongue around the tip, getting every little drop of that wonderful chocolate. Ooh, so good!

Let's do it again, ladies. But this time, keep your eyes closed as you dip your finger in the chocolate. Touch it to your lips, then leisurely flick your tongue out to lick the chocolate from your lips, before slowly inserting your finger into your mouth. Leave it there for just a moment, then slowly start stroking your finger in and out of your mouth – flicking it with your tongue each time it enters and leaves your lips.

Now, lastly, use your finger to dab a bit of chocolate slightly above and slightly below your lips. Now reach up with your tongue and lick the chocolate above your lips, then reach down for the chocolate below.

Eating chocolate has never been as sensuous has it? In addition to heightening your sense of taste, you've also been exercising your tongue. And you know every Sensuous Black Woman has to know how to use her tongue!

In fact, you should do this exercise every now and then to keep in practice, and each time you do put the chocolate a little higher above your lips until it's just under your nose, and a little lower under your lips until it's just above your chin. The more agile your tongue becomes the better.

Sense of Hearing
For this exercise you need a blindfold (preferably silk), a mixed tape or CD, and a

stereo system. Once again you need to turn off the electric lights, and light up some candles but also move the furniture so you have space to move around freely.

Place the tape or CD in the stereo (volume shouldn't be too loud), get comfortable on your couch, and place your blindfold over your eyes. Make sure it's not too tight because it shouldn't be distracting. Now lean back on the couch and relax, and listen to the music for a few minutes. Enjoy the tempo. Let it seep into your body. Lose yourself in the beat. Try to pick out the various instruments playing – the guitar, the keyboard, the drums, the horns. Feel the rough or smooth texture of the singer's voice, and let it wrap itself around you like a cocoon. Nestle in its warmth.

Sit there for at least two songs, relaxing and enjoying the music, but by the third cut I want you to stand up – still blindfolded – and let your body respond to the music. Don't worry about doing fancy dance steps, or any dance steps at all. You might simply want to sway back and forth or bop your head while raking your fingers through your hair. If you want to move around, please do so – if you simply want to gyrate or rub your hands over your body that's fine, too. The goal is to let the music seep inside your body and have it, and only it, dictate your actions.

3. <u>Sense of Touch</u>

For this exercise you'll need to be clad in only a pair of sexy panties. You'll also need a piece of fur, a piece of silk cloth, a peacock feather, an open chilled bottle of champagne, and a champagne glass. Lay your props on a table and get comfortable on the couch.

First, simply run your fingers over the fur, silk and peacock feather, lingering for at least thirty seconds on each of these items. Then pick up the fur, close your eyes, and bring it to your face – lightly stroking it over your forehead, eyes, and lips. Slowly, very slowly, bring it along your cheek, down the hollow of your throat, drawing it over your shoulders and chest, and down to your breasts – brushing it softly against your nipples – then down the middle of your breasts to your stomach, over your belly button, and finally down to your panty line. Then let the fur drop from your fingers onto the floor, and just lie on the couch reliving the experience in your mind. You should be able to feel the texture of the fur against your skin as if you were once again drawing it over your body.

Wait for a full minute, then do the same exercise with the silk and peacock feather.

Now sit up and pour the chilled champagne into the champagne glass. Don't drink yet! Take the glass and place it gently against your forehead, right below your hairline, and slowly bring it down in a straight line against the bridge of your nose, over your lips, down your chin to the hollow of your throat, between your breasts (don't touch your nipples!), and down to your belly button.

Then dip your finger into the cold champagne and, starting from your lips, slowly trace your finger back down to your belly button. Mmm!

Dip your finger in the champagne again but this time use it to rub first your right nipple, then your left, alternating until both nipples are hard. Now lay back and simply enjoy the sensation while drinking the rest of the champagne. Job well done!

4. <u>Total Senses</u>

This is the most fun of all the exercises. Put satin sheets on your bed (if you don't have satin sheets, you should get some. EVERYONE should have satin sheets – they just feel so good!), placing unscented talcum powder between the bottom sheet and the mattress cover. *Lightly* spray the sheets with your favorite cologne. Put a jazz CD in the stereo, and light two or three unscented candles.

Draw yourself a warm luxurious bath with bath salts and bubbles and have a glass of champagne and soft music playing in the bathroom, which should also be lit by candlelight. Ease yourself in the bath, close your eyes and just relax for a while as you leisurely sip your champagne, enjoying the sound of the music, the smell of the scented salts, and the warmth of the water. Use a sponge, not a washcloth, to clean and rinse yourself, then relax again before stepping out of the tub and gently blotting yourself with an extra fluffy towel.

Go into the bedroom and step in front of the mirror. Put a dab of lotion in the palm of your hands, and rub them together to warm the lotion, swaying to the music should you so desire. Slowly start massaging your throat, shoulders and arms with the lotion, then moving down to your breasts (replenish the lotion if need be), firmly cupping and massaging them. Look at your face in the mirror, and see how your own touch makes your face glow in the candlelight. Using more warmed lotion, now move down from your breasts to your stomach, your hips, and your buttocks. Now bend down and lotion your feet, your ankles, your calves, working your way back to your thighs so that you are once again in a standing position. Slightly open your legs apart, and move down from the top of your pubic hair to your vagina, opening your vaginal lips to also lotion around your clitoris – but don't touch your clit!

Now move to the bed, lay down, and stretch out on your back. Close your eyes, listen to the music, inhale the fragrance of the cologne, as you drift off to a blissful sleep. And should your hand start wandering again, well . . . enjoy!

Tuning Your Body

I'm not talking about gaining or losing weight here, I'm talking about making sure that you are physically at your peak, whatever your body shape might be.

Do you remember Fred Berry, who played "Rerun" in the television sitcom "What's Happening"? He was in his early twenties and well over two-hundred pounds when he first received national attention as a member of the Los Angeles dance group, the Lockers. He looked chubby, and stubby, but he could move like an acrobat. And if he could move like that on a dance floor, I can only imagine how he could move in bed. Makes me wet just thinking about it.

So, here's some suggestions on what you can do to tune-up your body and get in great sexual shape.

1. Take Dance Lessons

You don't have to go out and take ballet classes, but there's nothing wrong with taking a weekly African or Modern Dance class. It will help limber you up if you're not limber, and keep you limber if you are. Salsa classes are also good because it's one of the few dances still out that have you in physical contact with a partner so you can practice on relaxing and letting your man lead.. Also, find out if there's a Belly Dancing class being offered in your area – if so, hurry up and enroll. You'll learn some very sensuous moves!

2. Learn to Strip Tease

Uh-huh, that's right. Learn to do strip tease. Not only will you become skilled in a host of sensuous moves, but you'll discover strip-tease techniques that are guaranteed to turn a man on. One way to learn is visit strip-tease clubs and watch the girls in action. This way you can not only watch the girls in action, but also watch the reaction of the male customers so you can see what moves turn men on the most. Another alternative is to buy or rent a strip-tease video or DVD. I highly recommend "Carmen Electra's The Lap Dance & Hip Hop."

3. Practice Yoga

Yoga is actually a means of reducing stress as well as limbering your body. It's believed that yoga cleanses the body of toxins and improves the circulatory system and muscle tone. There are many different types of yoga, however with the exception of Power Yoga, most don't focus on aerobics, but instead focus on holding specific poses over a short period of time. Hatha is probably the most popular form of yoga, but I prefer Bikram, or Heat Yoga, which is done in a room with a temperature between ninety and one hundred degrees Fahrenheit. I find the heat helps stretch my muscles, and I can more easily maintain some of the required yoga positions.

The above are all suggested things you can do to get in tune with your body. Below are some musts!

4. Kegel Exercises

Ladies, whatever you do, don't disregard this step!

The Kegel Exercise was developed in 1948 by Dr. Arnold Kegel, a California gynecologist, to help correct incontinence in women. It wasn't long before it was discovered that the exercise can also greatly improve sexual performance! The Kegel Exercise is used to strengthen the pubococcygeus (PC) muscle which is the primary muscle used in sex. A strong pubococcygeus muscle can help you:

a. Reach orgasm easier!

b. Have better orgasms!

c. Heighten sensitivity in your vagina, leading to more sexual satisfaction!

d. Make your vagina tighter – meaning you can pull and squeeze your partner's penis better, thereby increasing his pleasure!

See why you need to learn how to do the exercise? Now pay close attention, because now I'll teach you how to do the exercise. Don't worry it's easy!

Ever had to pee really bad when there were no proper facilities around? The pubococcygeus muscle is the same muscle you use to hold it until you could find a toilet. Next time you go to the bathroom to urinate try to stop your urine mid flow, and pay attention to the muscle you contract to do so.

Okay, now that you've located the muscle, it's time to exercise it. First go empty your bladder. Okay, now you're ready. So, here we go.

1. Lay on the floor face up. Breathe slowly and deeply.

2. Put your hand on your stomach and squeeze your PC muscle. If you feel your abdominal muscles move, or if your buttocks or legs move, you're doing it wrong. Try again until you are isolating the PC muscle. Don't

worry if at first your rectum tenses too, after you've become adept at the Kegel Exercise you'll be able to squeeze the PC muscle without moving the anus muscle.

3. After you've isolated the PC muscle relax for a few moments.

4. Now, squeeze the PC muscle and slowly count to ten (one one-thousand, two one-thousand, etc.) then relax. When I say relax, it's important that you FULLY relax the muscle. (If you can't hold it for a ten count, don't worry. Do a six count, or four count, or whatever you can do. You'll eventually be able to do a ten count.)

5. Try to do ten sets of the exercise. If you can't do ten sets at first, don't worry. You'll eventually work up to it.

6. Repeat exercise three times a day. Once in the morning, once in the afternoon, and once in the evening.

After the first few times you won't have to lie on the floor to do your Kegel Exercise, you'll be able to do it while seated at your desk at work, while sitting in the waiting room of your doctor's office, or while standing in line at the supermarket. You should be able to see the difference in your sex life in just two to three weeks.

5. Learn Pelvic Thrusts

Pelvic thrusts are not only great for toning and tightening your butt, they also have the ability to improve your sexual performance. And HE won't be the only one who benefits, honey. A woman who is adept at pelvic thrusts can tilt her pelvic during sex to get maximum clitoral stimulation, and also make it easier for your partner's penis to reach her G-Spot (In case you don't know, and I'm always surprised when I find that so many women, don't, your G-spot is located *inside* the vagina, about 1 ½ inches up the anterior wall. It's rather difficult for a woman to reach it herself during masturbation). Pelvic thrusts are simple to do.

1. Lie on your back with your knees bent, hands at your side and palms face down on the floor.

2. Tense your arms and legs and pull your butt off the floor, squeezing your butt and PC muscles as you come up.

45

3. Hold for a count of ten then release.

4. Return to starting position.

Try to do three sets of twenty every day.

Wonderful, wonderful, wonderful! You're now in tune with your senses and your body. You're almost there, girlie! But now I want to take some time to talk to you about keeping your body clean and appealing.

Showers are all good and fine for men, but I believe that for a woman to be really clean she should bathe daily. Not only do baths feel great, they're also the best way to make sure that our precious privates are squeaky clean. Don't just rub down there with a wash cloth, open the hood of your clitoris and gently wipe down there with sudsy water to make sure you get out the bacteria that can build up there and promote body odor. But make sure you rinse well! Also, make sure you wash the inside of your ear because you never know when someone's going to want to stick his tongue in there!

Never go out without having feminine wipes in your pocketbook. Those are the things that look like big handy-wipes that you get at restaurants (at least the better ones) when you eat ribs or other finger foods. You can buy them in any drugstore or supermarket. Use them EVERYTIME you go to the bathroom, whether you do a number one or a number two. You never know when you're going to be involved in a "quickie," and you always want to be fresh as a daisy down there.

Always wear panty-liners. No matter how many times we douche, all women have a little vaginal discharge from time to time. A panty-liner will ensure that the odor doesn't get into the cloth of your underwear.

Make sure you take good care of your hands. Use hand lotion every day to keep them soft, because no man wants to feel calluses when you're stroking his cheeks. Your nails should always be neatly manicured, and you should never go out with chipped finger nail polish. And while a lot of us like to wear nail jewelry, it's been my experience that most men aren't necessarily turned on by them, and some are turned off. As for you ladies who like to wear three-inch fake talons, well, more power to you. But while they may be a conversation piece for your girlfriends, they are a definite turn-off for men. As one man told me, "Every time I see a chick with them long-ass nails I imagine her raking them across a blackboard, and I cringe. Ain't no way I'm going to let them shits anywhere near my bare back." Enough said.

And don't forget your feet! Do you know that the number one fetish with men is a foot fetish? That doesn't mean that all men want to suck your toes (but oh, it's wonderful when you find a man who does!), but they all do appreciate a set of good-looking feet. Pedicures are a must! And ladies, if you've never had a pedicure, you don't know what you're missing. It's one of the ultimate pampering experiences you'll ever have.

Keep your hair clean. Unlike white woman we don't wash our hair every day, but we should at least once a week, and more during the summer when the heat makes our scalp sweat. A man should never catch a whiff of an unseemly odor when nuzzling our hair. And cut down on the grease, girlfriends! No man wants a palm full of Dixie Peach or Posner's Bergamot after running his hand through our tresses. Yuck!

Body hair is a personal choice thing, but I personally like to keep my armpits and legs hairless. But if you do choose to have bushy armpits, PLEASE make sure that you wash under your arms not once a day, but at least twice!

So now that you've tuned up your confidence, your senses, and your body, you have one more thing to work on.

Tuning Your Attitude

It's all about the attitude, baby. It's all about the attitude.

Remember in my introduction (you did read my introduction, right?) I told you that when I first started studying Sensuous Black Women they seemed to give off the vibe, "I've got it going on and any man should be proud to have me on his arm. But I'm not giving myself to just any man," right? Well, none of them ever gave off the vibe that they were too good for any particular man. That's very important. They never acted like they were better than anyone else. In fact, Sensuous Black Women have a way of making every man feel special, like they really enjoy being around them. No matter how ugly, how broke, or how uneducated they are. They sent out a vibe that said they liked being around men, and that vibe made men want to be around them.

Sensuous Black Women walk around with their heads held high, but never with their noses in the air.

Let me put it another way. If you're one of those women who think other women hate you because they're jealous of your looks, you're wrong. They hate you because you're a bitch.

A Sensuous Black Woman has a pleasant and inviting attitude that draws people – men and women – to her; never an attitude that says she thinks she's better than anyone else.

I've said it before, and I'll say it again – men enjoy women they believe enjoy them. Women who they think find them interesting.

Learn how to listen to people, show them you appreciate them. At the very least throw them an occasional but genuine smile now and then.

And you know what? If you take just a few moments to get to know someone you'll find that you're not faking it. Every man, and woman, has something interesting about them. One of the talents that Sensuous Black Women must possess is the ability to find out what that interesting thing is, and allow the other person to see that they're interested. You've got to learn to make every man, whether it's someone you are interested in pursuing or not, feel as if they're important. There is simply nothing more appealing.

The only way to tune your attitude is to improve your attitude toward people. This is essential to becoming the Sensuous Black Woman.

Got that?

Okay, you are now prepared to start your new life as the Sensuous Black Woman. Excited? Good! Because now we're finally going to cover the techniques every Sensuous Black Woman needs.

Read on, Sista! Read on!

Smart Flirting – Or How to Catch That Fish!

I never did like Daphne. Not even when we were in the sixth grade in P.S. 22 in the Bronx and she was the darling of all the teachers who somehow didn't know she was screwing half the boys in the class. She was one of those kids who acted like an angel around grown-ups while poking fun at them behind their backs. Actually, it wasn't only adults with whom she was hypocritical. She should have pursued a career as a knife-thrower at the circus. She was that good at stabbing people in the back.

I really started disliking her when she started screwing my best friend's boyfriend, and threw it up in her face at one of those basement parties that we all used to attend back in the seventies. But Constance was one of the ridiculously all-forgiving girls, and within a few months they started hanging out again. And since I hung with Constance, I too often found myself in the company of that slut Daphne.

Some years later, I stopped over at Constance's house one evening when she, Daphne, and a couple of other girls were getting ready to go to a dance. They were all talking about a guy from Brooklyn who had just been drafted by the New Jersey Nets and who was going to be there.

"Yeah, I heard he got a big signing bonus," one of the girls said as she plastered her face with Cover Girl foundation that was two shades too light.

"And I heard he just broke up with his girl friend," Daphne said as she twirled in front of the mirror. "So you'd better believe that he's coming home with me tonight. I need someone who can afford to show me the finer things in life. I saw a pair of leather boots I've been dying for."

"What makes you think you can snag him?" Constance asked.

"What makes you think I can't?" Daphne answered in her little snotty voice. Then she shot Constance a look that said, 'you should know better than anyone else, bitch.' I decided right then and there I was going to go to that dance.

There was already a crowd gathered around the basketball player by the time we got to the dance, but Daphne made a beeline toward him anyway. I watched as she batted her eyes and wiggled her skin tight mini-skirted ass while she told him that she had been following his career since his high school days. He was polite, but I was hoping he'd ask if she knew what high school he'd attended since I knew she didn't. She managed to get a seat next to him and I watched as she crossed and uncrossed her legs, leaned over him so far that her boobs almost fell out and giggled every time he said anything, to her or anyone else at the table.

"Looks like Daphne's going to get those boots," Constance whispered in my ear.

"The night's still young," I whispered back.

Turns out Daphne didn't get those boots, but I did get a brand new Mercedes Benz a few months later, courtesy of the newest power forward for the New Jersey Nets.

There's a definite fine art to flirting, and poor Daphne didn't have a clue. I, on the other hand, have mastered the art. Keep reading, and so will you.

First off, let's start with clothing. Sexy lingerie is a must. Not because you're going to be jumping into bed with the guy at that first meeting, but because when you wear sexy undies you simply feel sexy. So forget those $1.50 panties on sale at Walmart, start shopping at Victoria's Secret. Grab some sexy lace bra and panty sets, and a couple of silk numbers, too! You'll thank yourself later when you find yourself sensually slinking into parties instead of just strolling in like everyone else.

I know we were raised in the age of pantyhose, but while you're at Victoria Secrets, consider getting a few pairs of stockings and a couple of garter belts. You'll never want to go back to pantyhose, honey. Not only do stockings simply make you feel sexy, they're also a lot easier to put on – and they make a man go wild when you take them off in front of him. And there's nothing more sensuous than seeing a lone stocking casually strewn across the back of a bedroom chair.

We all want to look sexy when we go out, and we should, but remember there's a difference between looking sexy and looking like a whore. Dress like a hoochie-mama and you're going to be treated like a hoochie mama. While I love to wear short dresses and skirts to show off my legs, I don't wear anything so short that I'm in danger of flashing my butt cheeks when I'm walking, or so tight I can't cross my legs when I sit down. There's never an excuse to wear clothes that don't fit perfectly.

If you have cleavage you want to show it off (and if you don't have cleavage, buy push-up bras so you do), but you don't want to go around wearing outfits that will put you at risk of a wardrobe malfunction.

And keep in mind what's going on beneath the clothing that also makes you feel as sexy and sensuous. Ever heard of a bikini wax? Ever thought about getting one? The traditional bikini wax only removes hair that might be visible while wearing a traditional bikini. A Brazilian bikini wax gets rid of everything. The procedure is far from painless (it involves wax being put on your most private parts, and then removed with the YANK of linen cloth), but boy does it make you feel sexy afterward!

So now that you're dressed for success, let's get down to business!

There is a huge difference between outrageous flirting and smart flirting. Daphne was a very obvious and outrageous flirt. Everyone within a ten mile radius could see what she was doing, and judge her performance as well as her morals. What YOU need to learn is smart flirting – being so subtle that most of the people around won't pick up on your plan, and the man you're targeting doesn't even realize he's a mark. The goal is to make him so intrigued by you that he goes after you.

Got it?

Okay, the four most important things you need to remember for smart flirting are the following:

1. Body Language

2. Eye Contact

3. Conversation

4. Touch

Body Language and Eye Contact
Do you remember your mother telling you "You should always make a good first impression?" Well, the admonishment certainly holds true for flirting. When you walk into a room, before people notice your face, your hair, or your clothes, they notice how you walk in. Don't believe me? Think about this. The first time I saw a woman wearing the new retro afro-hairstyle – the one where the hair is natural, and looks like a really uncombed afro – I looked at

her and thought, 'Hell if she doesn't look like something the cat dragged in. She looks a hot mess.' Then I was partying at a Los Angeles club and in walked Macy Gray, and I thought, 'damn, is she wearing that hair or what?'" The way you walk in sets the tone of how people will appraise you. If you strut in head high, shoulders back, with a little sway to your walk you're projecting "I got it going on," people will assess your appearance accordingly.

When you're going out to make contacts, or to snag a man, you shouldn't stroll into a room as much as you should make an entrance. Keep your head high and shoulders back so that people will actually have to look up at you, and move purposely, but not hurriedly, your pelvic thrust forward as you walk

Keep a slight smile on your lips as you casually peruse the room, and when you spot a target, wait until you make eye contact, then let the smile disappear for a beat, and then let it slowly reappear, holding the eye contact no less than two seconds, but no more than three. Then turn away from him and focus your attention on someone else. Anyone else. This signals the man that while you're basically just a friendly person, he so impressed you that you were taken aback, and had to regain your composure.

But then, and this is important, position yourself so that while your face is turned toward the person you're now talking to, your body is at least partially turned toward your target. If you have a drink in your hand, it should be in the hand that is closest to your targeted man. For even greater effect, tinkle the ice in the drink. Even if he's too far away to hear the tinkle, he'll be able to imagine he does, and subconsciously respond to it as if it were the come hither signal that it is. But don't worry if he doesn't rush over, you're only just getting started.

If you're sitting down, keep your legs pointed toward your targeted man, and dangle a shoe from one foot in his direction. Another come hither signal. If you're wearing shoes with straps, let some other piece of your clothing casually dangle in his direction – but it must seem like an unconscious action for it to be effective. I love to wear shawls, and my favorite move is to let the shawl fall down over one shoulder, the shoulder nearest my target. If all fails, play with your earring. This all gives the target man the subconscious impression that you're undressing for him, and him only. Another turn-on!

Important note, while it's a great idea to cross your legs (if you can't cross them at the thigh, at least cross them at the ankle) do NOT cross your arms. This signals that you're unavailable. Definitely not the impression you want to give.

No less than three minutes after making that initial eye contact, gaze back over to him, and as soon as his eyes meet yours lower your eyes for half a second, raise them again to meet his, then quickly lower them again and turn away and talk to someone else.

Now keep in mind that it takes time to perfect these moves, so please don't be discouraged if it doesn't work for you the first, second or third time. Remember that other little saying of your mother's, "Practice makes perfect."

And of course there's always the chance that you simply don't appeal to the man. Don't take it personally! Even Tyra Banks can't snag every man she sets her sights on. And if you've followed my instructions to the tee, you have no need to be embarrassed – most of the people around you aren't intuitive enough to pick up your subtle flirting moves. It's only if you're an outrageous flirt that people will snicker that you've had your face cracked.

So if after all these moves your target man doesn't find his way to where you're sitting or standing, you have a choice. You can either move closer to him or cut your losses and focus on someone else. If you casually walk over close to him and he doesn't initiate conversation with you, my advice is to go ahead and leave it alone. He's just not into you – his loss not yours. After all, he just missed out on getting to know a truly Sensuous Black Woman. But whatever you do, don't continue going after him, no matter how much you might want to. Because if you do, you've set the tone of your entire future relationship. There's an old French saying – in every relationship there's the person who kisses, and the person who allows themselves to be kissed. As a Sensuous Black Woman, YOU should be the one on the receiving end of those kisses, sweetie.

Conversation and Touch

Once you've gotten your target to come over to where you are, look at him and flash him a big smile. That's his reward – at least for now. If he doesn't introduce himself to you it's okay for you to introduce yourself to him. Reach out and shake his hand when he tells you his name, and don't make it a limp handshake, but not too firm either. You don't want to come off like a helpless female, but you don't want to come off like you're competing for the masculine role either. IMPORTANT – when he says his name, repeat it after him. This gives him the impression that he's significant enough to you for you to make it a point to remember his name.

Now dear, oh dear, what to talk about? Well, in order for you to truly be a Sensuous Black Woman, you have to be well-read and well-spoken. Even if you aren't up-to-date on the classics, you should at least be up-to-date with current events. If all else fails you can always fall back on what's going on in the news, right?

Let the man lead the conversation. Don't try to impress him with your smarts or wit, just follow his lead. Don't laugh at his jokes if they're not funny – it takes great practice to realistically fake a laugh – but do smile. And when he does crack a truly funny joke, then reward him with a tingly laugh. Ask him questions about himself – after all, a man's favorite subject is himself. Make sure the questions are open-ended rather than ones that require only a "yes" or "no" answer. The more you keep him talking the more you'll find out about him, and the more he'll be fascinated by you. Why? Because he thinks you're fascinated by him!

Now here's the thing. While you're talking to the man maintain steady eye contact, but not to the point of staring. This shows him that you're very interested in him and what he's saying, but it also gives you an opportunity to find out just how interested he is. If he finds you really intriguing his pupils will be dilated. It's unconscious, so he can't fake it.

If he finds you intriguing, and you find him intriguing, now you have to totally reel him in.

While you're talking to him, play with your hair, and more importantly go for the throat. Yours, not his.

Take your drink, or your fingers, and slowly (and seemingly unconsciously) trail them down your throat while he's talking to you. Not while you're talking, because then it looks fake. This is a move that most men can't resist. Why? Because if you think about it, the throat is the one part of the exposed body that is still off limits to people. A man can "accidentally" brush your face, your arms or your legs, but how can he accidentally brush your throat? By seductively touching it in front of him it gives him the impression that if he plays his cards right he might soon be able to touch it, too.

Now it's time for you to actually reach out and touch him. Your hands are well lotioned and your nails are manicured, right? Good. I want you to take your hand – while you're talking, not him – and casually, and very softly, place it on his. Keep it on for three seconds, long enough for him to notice it but not long enough to make it seem purposeful, then remove it as if you didn't even realize you had touched him in the first place. Make sure you're smiling, and you're speaking about a pleasant subject when you do this. You want him to associate your touch with pleasantness. But don't do it while complimenting him. It would then seem purposeful. Try to do this at least twice during a ten minute conversation. You should also try to casually touch the trunk of his body. You can accomplish this by softly brushing your hand over his shoulder to remove an imaginary piece of lint. The important thing is to always keep your touch soft, and feminine.

Find a reason to whisper something in his ear. It could be something like, "See that woman at the bar? She looks just like my Aunt Gertrude." Lean in close to him to make the whisper, and if you softly brush his ear with your lips so much the better. Men love to hear a woman whisper, no matter what it is they're saying. Because what HE"S hearing is "she's opening her soul to me."

Congratulations! At this point your fish should be hooked. But now just a few miscellaneous tips.

1. As soon as you're sure you have his nose open, make yourself unavailable. Tell him you believe you see someone you know, and say you have to go over and talk to him or her. Stay away about ten minutes, long enough for him to realize he misses you. Also, try not to spend more than an hour with him at your first meeting. Always leave him wanting more.

2. Don't do something nice for him until he does something nice for him. You'll thank me for this tip later on in your relationship. He has to learn early on that he should be the giver, and you the very appreciative receiver.

3. If you're flirting with two men at once, and I wouldn't recommend this until you've had a lot of practice, make sure that each one thinks he's the only one you're interested in. If you're on a dance floor with one and the song goes off and the other man then takes your hand for the next dance, flash your first partner a wistful smile that says, "oh, I'm sorry. I'd really rather be with you." And after he walks off, turn and flash your new partner a smile that says, "Thanks so much for saving me. You're the one I really wanted to be with."

4. When you go out flirting don't sit or stand around a lot of women. Your target might not approach you for fear of you rejecting him in front of your friends.

5. If you've targeted one man, and another man (whom you're not the least bit attracted to) comes on to you, don't reject him harshly. Your target might be watching and decide not to risk the same fate. Be kind in turning the unwanted fellow away.

And now just a couple of tips on flirting etiquette.

Don't ever flirt with one of your friends' man. Not even for practice. Nothing can ruin a friendship quicker.

Don't flirt with a man you're truly not interested in. It's just not nice, and no one likes a tease.

So now that you've met and hooked your man it's time to learn about how to keep him not only satisfied, but also wild about you. What you've got to do is totally and completely turn him out -- you've got to treat him like he's never before been treated by a woman. And the next couple of chapters will teach you how to do exactly that.

So read on, ladies . . . read on!

How To Drive Him Wild In Bed

He was suave, handsome, well-dressed and the greatest lover I'd ever been with in with my life. And wouldn't you know his name was Romeo? All the girls were crazy about him, including me.

I was a silly, giggly seventeen-year-old when I first saw him. I was at a party with my girlfriends when those dreamy bedroom eyes caught my attention.

"Who's he?" I asked one of my girlfriends.

"Bad news," she told me with a smirk. "Don't bother with him. He's one of those love 'em and leave 'em guys. A real heartbreaker."

"But boy can he fuck your brains out," another girl added. "Problem is he never comes back for seconds."

I found out how right she was when I ran into Romeo in the supermarket a couple of months later. He was in the produce section, and I kind of sidled over hoping he'd ask me to help him pick out a head of lettuce or something. That's how it always happened in the Hollywood movies, right? Well, it didn't work that day in real life. He acted as if he didn't even see me. I discretely followed him to the frozen food section, the dairy section, and then finally to the check-out counter. By this time I was desperate.

"Hi," I said just before he gave the cashier his platinum credit card. "Didn't we meet at a party a couple of months ago? You know, the one on 169th Street."

His brow furrowed as if trying to remember.

"We actually met?" he finally asked.

"Well, we didn't actually meet." I gave a self-conscious smile. "But I saw you there. Your name is Romeo, right?"

"Uh-huh," he answered rather skeptically.

"That's what I thought. Do you live around here?"

"No, I'm just doing some shopping for my grandmother. She lives around the corner."

Wow. He can't be all that bad if he's shopping for his poor sick grandmother, I thought. Maybe my friends were wrong. I was even more convinced they were wrong after we had a cup of coffee at a nearby restaurant. Romeo was sweet, funny, and seemed like a really decent and caring guy. My friends were probably jealous because they'd never been able to get with him, I decided.

We didn't stay at the restaurant long because he had some additional errands to run for his grandmother, but we exchanged telephone numbers and he promised to call the next day. It was a week later before I finally got the courage to call him.

"Hi," I said nervously when he picked up the phone. "I hate to bother you because I guess you've been busy and all, but I was wondering if you might want to go to the movies tomorrow. My friend works at the AMC theater downtown, and she can get us in for free.

He kind of chuckled and said, "I've got a better idea. I have two tickets for a Broadway play tomorrow evening. Wanna go?"

We had a great time. He never explained why he had never gotten around to calling me, and I didn't ask. I was too busy enjoying myself. He took me for an early dinner before the play, then he took me to a club for a couple of drinks, after the play. Then he brought me home and completely turned me out! He started out by taking my face in his hands, then kissing me on the forehead, nose and than on the mouth. Then when I was turned on beyond belief he took me into the bedroom and undressed me. I never had anyone undress me before. And oh he made love to me like I'd never been made love to before. We did it on the bed, on the floor, on the kitchen table and even on the windowsill. He was very well-endowed and very well skilled. All I could really do was lay back and enjoy. I was in heaven! Then unlike some cads who get their shit off and then get up and leave, Romeo actually spent the night and held me while I slept. How romantic! I just knew I'd found the perfect man.

I got up early the next morning and fixed him breakfast, then he gave me a long soulful kiss, said he'd call me later that day, and split to go to work.

After six months of leaving messages on his answering machine with no return calls, I finally realized that my girlfriends were right. Except he wasn't a normal dog who would just love 'em and leave 'em, Romeo was one of those guys who would take the time to make sure that he had a woman loving him before he walked out on her. He was worse then a dog. He was a damn Romeo.

I didn't run into him again for nearly three years. It was at an after-party for a well-known gangsta rap artist, and of course I was surrounded by a bunch of men vying for my attention. I had spotted Romeo as soon as I walked in, but I quickly looked away before he noticed me. I waited until I had a drink in my hand and was heartily laughing at a joke that one of my admirers made when I casually looked over at Romeo again. As soon as I caught his eye, I momentarily stopped laughing, and looked at him as if I were trying to place him, then put a very pleasant smile on my face and raised my glass in his direction then turned back to my admirer and focused my full attention on him. Of course I put my drink to the hollow of my neck, and lightly fluffed my hair as I pretended to be engrossed with whatever the hell it was he was saying.

I was careful not to look in Romeo's direction again, but I secretly smiled to myself as I noticed him discretely following me around the party the same way I had followed him around the supermarket all those years before. It took almost an hour, but he finally sidled up to me.

"So, it's been quite some time, huh? How are you doing, lady?" He asked me with a sexy smile on his face.

I squinted my eyes when I looked up at him. "Romeo, right?" I said, pretending I had to try and remember his name. "I've been fine. What about you? What have you been up to?"

He went into this long monologue about how he was managing this new rap star, and they were on the road so much he never had time to even catch up with his friends in the city. I guess this was his half-ass attempt to "explain" why he'd never contacted me again. I just smiled real pretty, and said, "That must be so exciting, managing rap artists." That was all the encouragement he needed. He took a seat next to me and just went on and on with stories about his glamorous life. I smiled and nodded, but then after a half hour I faked a small yawn and looked at my watch. "My goodness, I didn't realize it was so late."

I picked up my clutch bag and stood up, then slowly bent over him and kissed his cheek. "You smell very nice," I said as I straightened back up. "Oh aren't those earrings nice," I said pointing to a beautiful girl who walked by. "I think they're real emeralds. But listen, it was really nice running into you. Good luck with your artist." I started to head for the door, but he put his hand on my arm to stop me.

"Listen, my car is parked right outside. Let me give you a ride," he said with his confident smile.

My return smile was just as confident as I said, "That's okay. I'm parked right outside, too. But thanks for the offer."

"Well, can I follow you home so we can talk about old times?" His voice was losing some of his confidence now.

Mine wasn't. "No, I really have to get up early so I need to get some sleep."

"Well, can I get your telephone number? Maybe we can go out for dinner later this week."

We exchanged numbers and I headed out, but not before I stopped and talked to a couple of more men, and very noticeably took their telephone numbers.

When I arrived home an hour later there was a voice mail message from Romeo waiting for me, telling me how glad he was that we had reconnected and that he was looking forward to seeing me again soon. Wasn't that sweet? So were the other six messages I received from him over the next week. Of course I didn't return any of the calls.

I finally called him ten days after the party and told him that I'd been sooooo very busy, but I was really looking forward to seeing him, and asked if we could possibly get together for dinner the next evening.

The restaurant he picked out was exquisite – candlelight, violin players, the works. The man really knew how to set the mood. But then again, he was a Romeo.

We went back to my apartment afterward, and Romeo went through about twenty minutes of small talk before he finally made his move. He took my face in his hands, looked deep into my eyes, then gently kissed me on the forehead, then the nose, and finally gave me a long passionate kiss on the lips. I faked a soft moan, and half-heartedly tried to move away from him, but of course he simply pulled me closer and kissed me again. This time I gave a slight whimper and started gyrating my pelvic against him as if I was losing control.

"I can't believe how good you make me feel," I said in short gasps.

"I want to make you feel even better," he said as he massaged my back with one hand while unbuttoning my blouse with the other. "I need to make you feel better." With that I let him lead me to my bedroom.

He took his time undressing me, and when he was finished and I was standing naked in front of him, I suddenly put one arm across my breast and covered my pubic area with the other.

"You don't think we're going to fast," I said in my most hesitant voice as I slightly backed away from him.

"No, baby," he said, pulling me back to him and into a kiss.

I let out another whimper and let my body relax against him in subtle form of surrender, but surrender was the last thing on my mind.

While he massaged my back and ran his fingers through my hair I undid the top buttons of his shirt and gently nuzzled the silky chest hairs that peeked out above his undershirt while I finished unbuttoning the shirt. I then pushed up his undershirt and begin licking and softly nibbling his nipples, slowly working down to just above his belt line. I was rewarded with the same moans I had just been giving him, only I knew his were genuine. Just a few minutes later I was on my knees in front of him, and he was almost swooning.

I turned him out but good. We went four rounds that night, and each time I let him initiate it and let him think he was in control for a few minutes, then acted like he had me so turned on so much that I was transformed into an insatiable wild woman who couldn't keep my hands, and my mouth off of him. Right before he slipped off to sleep I kissed him on the cheek and then whispered "thank you" in his ear.

"What are you thanking me for?" he asked sleepily.

"For fucking me so good," I answered as I settled into his arms. "I've never had a man as good as you."

He didn't call me once the next day. He called three times. Each time I let my answering machine pick up. I did the same when he called me four times the day after. He stopped calling for a while, but then his calls resumed after another three days. I waited one more day before I called him. After we had dinner that night he pulled a small jewelry box from his pocket. I opened it up and gasped. Inside were a pair of emerald earrings like the one I had admired at the party. I took him home and amply rewarded him.

I strung him along for another two months, and received a necklace and ring to match those emerald earrings, then dropped him as unceremoniously as he had dropped me three years previously, before I became a Sensuous Black Woman.

How did I turn the tables? Well, I used most of the flirting techniques we talked about in my previous chapter to initially intrigue him, but it was my bedroom antics that hooked him for good. You see instead of simply laying back to enjoy Romeo's skills as I had done when we first got together, I became an active (very active!) participant in our lovemaking. I used every trick in the book on him, and made some up as I went along. But the real trick was allowing him to think that it was him who was the real lover, and that it was his expertise that inspired me to such great heights. That fed into

his ego, and men like Romeo have huge egos –
thanks to the many women who swoon at their
feet like I had previously done.

Each man is different, so it's up to you to
figure out exactly what you need to do to hook
him.

Some men want you to take control from
the very beginning. Other men want women
who are totally submissive in bed. And many
men, like Romeo, want to think they're in
control but in reality want women who can turn
them out.

Practice will allow you to easily
differentiate between these types of men, and
then treat them according to their type.
Remember – and this is important – desire
begins in the mind. If you want to drive a man
wild in bed you have to know how to make love
to his mind and ego.

But moving beyond all of that, I think
it's about time we start talking about the more
physical aspects of sex and lovemaking.
Wouldn't you say?

I.   In Order For You To Be Good at Sex, You Have To Enjoy Sex!

The first thing I want to talk to you about
are orgasms – yours, not his.

Did you know that studies show that only about 40 percent of women say they've reached orgasm during sexual intercourse? I was blown away when I read this, and really found it hard to believe, but even my informal surveys support these statistics. On the other hand, most women who masturbate (and I believe all women should!) do achieve orgasm so it seems we're much better at taking matters into our own hands rather than finding ways to share our bliss.

Now let me say that there are some women who will never experience orgasm during intercourse, but let me also say that I believe that a significant amount more women would achieve it if they learned how to do so – for instance, learning what positions or techniques they need to use, or have their partner use, to make it happen. I mean, come on, let's face it – it would be nice to depend on your partner to make sure you climax, but we all know that most men are all about getting their own shit off. It's up to YOU to make sure you get yours.

So the first thing you have to do is educate yourself on orgasms.

And to start off, let me tell you that the three common ways for a woman to reach orgasm is through:

1. Clitoral Stimulation

2. G-Spot Stimulation

3. Vaginal Intercourse

1. Clitoral Stimulation

Ladies, it's time for you to get naked and grab a hand mirror. It's time you took a visual tour of your . . . um . . . your pussy – aka, your vulva.

Yeah, that's right. We're about to do some exploring!

First off, you'll see the "outer labia," which we commonly call our lips. That's the part of your pussy that's covered with pubic hair and overlays your clitoris and your vagina.

Then there's the "hood" and the "inner labia." These are what many women erroneously think is their clitoris. The hood is the bit of overhang that is connected to the inner labia. The inner labia resembles a second set of lips, but is significantly thinner and made of tissue rather than normal flesh. The inner labia starts at the hood and extends down to the vaginal opening. Some women's inner labia (especially those of African-American women) will slightly extend outside the outer labia, but not always.

If you open the inner labia you'll see a shaft (looks like a shallow tunnel) that extends from the top of the inner labia down to the vaginal opening. At the top of the inner labia, right below the hood, there's a small projection of tissue-like flesh. That's your clitoris!

And the small pink spot located at the very tip of the clitoris is the clitoral glans, or love button. Keeping the inner labia lips open simply take the tip of your finger and touch it. Chances are a tingling sensation will quickly run through your body. That's the part of your vulva (pussy?) that is the most sensitive, and which needs to be stimulated in order for you to reach a clitoral orgasm.

Since the clitoris is – for the most part – hidden, you might question how it can be stimulated during intercourse. Well, when a woman is aroused the clitoris becomes enlarged and will often extend beyond the inner labia so it can be massaged and stimulated by your partner's pubic area rubbing against it as he's thrusting inside of you. But some sexual positions are better for this than others (We'll get into sexual positions later in this chapter.).

Of course if your partner is a considerate lover he'll make sure your clitoris is stimulated even if it means playing with it during sex. But if not, there's nothing wrong with you playing with yourself during sex. In fact, most men get a kick out of watching a woman play with her clitoris during sex – they feel like you're putting on a show just for them. Some men will actually move your hand in position to do so. Go for it, honey!

Of course if you're shy, you can always resort to simply masturbating behind closed doors. In fact, I believe every woman should indulge in a healthy regime of masturbation. (I might even write another book on that subject alone!)

2. G-Spot Stimulation

The G-Spot is named after Dr. Ernst Grafenberg, a Berlin gynecologist who wrote about this erogenous zone back in 1950. It wasn't until 1980, however, when the book "The G-Spot" was written by Beverly Whipple, that most people were made aware of its existence.

This wonderful spot is located about 1 ½ inches inside the vagina on the anterior (front) wall. The exact placement may vary a bit, but imagine that you have a clock inside your vagina, with 12 o'clock pointed toward your navel – your G-Spot will be somewhere between 11 and 1 o'clock. Many women can reach it with their index finger if they position themselves so their legs are open wide giving themselves maximum penetration. If not, you can definitely reach it with a vibrator. It's about the size of a small pea, but when you're aroused it's increased to the size of a walnut.

Unlike the clitoris, just touching the G-Spot won't result in orgasm, but continuous stimulation can result in the most powerful orgasm you've ever experienced.

4. Vaginal Intercourse

Though most women need direct stimulation to their clitoris or G-Spot, there are others who can simply get off through regular vaginal intercourse. The deeper the penetration by the man, the more likely it is that a woman will achieve a vaginal orgasm.

*Female Orgasm and Ejaculation

Yep. It's true. Not all, but many women actually ejaculate during orgasm. Unfortunately, a lot of women don't realize this, and this lack of knowledge will actually stop them from reaching orgasm!

Let me explain.

Although the G-Spot is not the only way to achieve orgasm, many women say that their first experience with ejaculation was associated with a G-Spot orgasm. They also say that when the spot is being stimulated, just before they reach orgasm, they feel as if they have to urinate. This feeling usually passes in somewhere between five and ten seconds, but many women will suppress their orgasm because they are afraid they'll "pee" on themselves and embarrass themselves in front of their partner!

The reason women will momentarily feel as if they need to urinate might be because the bladder and the G-Spot are located only inches away from each other. But if you let yourself relax and go with the orgasm instead of holding yourself back you'll find that female ejaculation is definitely not urine, even though the ejaculation is ejected from your urethra rather than your vagina. Female ejaculation is almost clear in color, and has little or no odor and it's virtually tasteless. There's no reason to be embarrassed by it, whether you're by yourself or with a man. In fact, men are usually turned on by women who ejaculate – it's physical proof that they are able to make a woman "cum like mad."

So ladies, just go with the flow!

I just can't stress this enough – you *have to* learn to enjoy sex before you can learn how to give good sex. You've *got to* enjoy your own orgasm before you can really enjoy bringing a man to his. It's all about being in tune with your sensuality ladies! And after all, why should he get more out of it than you?

II. Setting the Mood!

If you don't know by now, you should know, candlelight is a woman's best friend when it comes to setting the mood. First of all, it's sensuous; and second of all, EVERY woman looks good when bathed in candlelight.

We've talked about candles in the bathroom and in the bedroom, but it's just as sensuous in the dining and living room.

So when you invite him over for "drinks" make sure you have at least seven or eight candles in the living room – you don't need as many in the bedroom, but you should have more light in the living room so as not to seem too obvious! You can also have one or two table lamps if you feel you need even more light but if you do, make sure to put a dark cloth over the lamp shade to dim the brightness. But caution here . . . don't put the cloth directly on the lamp or you'll create a fire hazard. It might also be good to remember to blow out the candles before you retire to the bedroom.

Use scented candles – specifically cinnamon scented candles. Why? Because cinnamon scent is a sexual turn on for men. Yes, I know it sounds stupid, but study after study has shown this to be true, and my own personal experience with seduction has borne it out. Cinnamon doesn't do anything for me or for most women, but since it does something for men, use it! Just as a personal tip, not only do I use cinnamon scented candles when entertaining men, I also empty a bottle of cinnamon in a pot of water and let it steam on the stove to make sure the smell totally permeates the house.

So now we know how your house should smell. How should you smell? First of all, I'm one of those people who believe that a woman should find her perfect scent and stick with it. No changing perfumes from one night, or one month, to the next. Every woman should have a signature scent, so that when a man smells it anywhere he thinks of you. HOWEVER, when you're ready to do the nasty, I want you to get a little nasty.

Ever heard of pheromones? They are natural chemicals produced by living organisms that affect other members of the same species. Sex pheromones attract the opposite gender of a species. They're so irresistible they are actually used as an ingredient in pesticides to lure insects to their deaths.

And a human woman's sexual pheromone is just as irresistible to a human man!

So here's a little sex tip for you, dear sistas!

Before your man comes over for your arranged tryst, bathe yourself thoroughly with scented oils and bath beads, then just after you towel yourself off and before you get dressed, stick your finger inside your vagina and then dab the vaginal juice behind your ears, on your wrists, and the base of your throat; just as you would perfume.

Take my word for it . . . it works!

How about another little tip?

After you've done your little dip and dab, take a Lifesaver™, and stick it in down there. Uh huh, I'm serious. Placing a Lifesaver™ in your vagina makes your coochie taste like candy when your man goes down on you. Boy, will he be shocked, and oh so pleased! I guarantee he'll stay down there a lot longer than he used to!

Cherry Lifesavers™ seem to be men's preferred taste (based on my own informal survey), but unless you're going to pop right into bed after you put it in you might want to choose pineapple. Why? Because if you're not having sex right away the Lifesaver™ will begin to melt and leave a slight stain in their panties. And who wants a red stain in their panties? Pineapple and lemon Lifesavers™ leave a faint yellow stain that's barely noticeable, but men (again based on my informal survey) prefer the taste of pineapple over lemon.

What do you wear for sex? It depends on the man. Some men like their women naked, some prefer nighties or teddies. Experiment to find out what your man likes. Wearing stockings and a garter belt (and maybe even your high heels) is a turn on for a lot of men, but this really only works if you're doing it doggy-style.

Have music playing. Some of you might be hip-hop fans, or rock and roll or R&B fans, but let me tell you something, nothing sets the mood like light jazz. And make sure it's an instrumental piece. Why? Because you don't want the man to get caught up in the lyrics – you don't want them to "read" into the words of say a love song and think you have love on your mind rather than lovemaking. You don't want them to think you're trying to trap them into a relationship, especially if you are. The opposite is true when a man is setting the mood for a woman, by the way . . . then he wants to play love songs, if only to subliminally suggest to her he's interested in love rather than just lovemaking.

And having jazz CDs make you seem sophisticated. Get familiar with the jazz greats like John Coltrane (my favorite mood piece by him is "Afro Blue) Dave Brubeck (try his cut "Take Five") Thelonious Monk (go for "Blue Bolivar Blues) if you want to impress a real jazz enthusiast (He doesn't have to know you only play them when you're setting the mood, right?). But even men who aren't necessarily into jazz like hearing it as background music.

Have condoms handy. Nothing breaks the mood like having to run out to the drugstore in order to buy rubbers. And sistas, my dear sistas, there is absolutely NO excuse for not practicing safe sex. NONE! Do you believe that if you insist a man wear a condom he'll walk out on you? Then hand him his hat and coat and escort him to the door. If he doesn't care about his own safety there's something wrong with him anyway, and any man who doesn't care about *your* safety you just don't need.

Once a man physically hands you a clean bill of health from a clinic you still have to be in a monogamous relationship with him for a minimum of six months and then send him back for another clean bill of health before you can consider having unprotected sex with him.

And don't listen to lame excuses like "My dick is too big I can't find condoms that fit." A regular size condom can actually fit over your hand and roll down to your forearm. I doubt your man's penis is larger than that. But just in case, (ha, ha, hah!) they do make condoms in larger sizes (and smaller sizes for those men who are not so generously endowed.)

By the way ladies, you should know a little something something about those novelty condoms you love to buy for your men. You know the glow in the dark kind? Or the peppermint flavored kind? Well, they're the most likely to break, leaving you at risk for pregnancy or STD's. Stick with latex condoms, please? And it's best to buy the latex condoms made in the United States, because some countries are marketing condoms made of inferior latex, which are also prone to breaking.

And if your man uses the excuse that he'll lose his erection in the time it takes to put the condom on, well . . . there's a solution to that. Put it on for him, using your mouth. I bet your man will stay hard then!

And here's how!

1. Get your man naked, and standing or sitting in front of you. Kiss him passionately, and give him an "Oh boy, you're in for a treat smiled.

2. Carefully open the condom package, being very careful not to tear the latex.

3. Put a small dab of water-based lubricant on the tip of his penis (just the tip, mind you.), looking up at him lovingly while you do so.

4. Place the condom in your mouth – behind your teeth – using a bit of suction to keep it in place.

5. Hold the shaft of his penis in one hand, and lower your mouth to the head of his penis and allow the condom to rest on the tip.

6. Let up slightly on the suction, and push the condom down his penis with your mouth. Keep your lips over your teeth so you don't accidentally hurt him. Your lips will need the strength of your teeth behind them to push the condom down quickly.

7. The first few times you try this technique you probably will not be able to get the condom all the way down the penis shaft. Don't worry about it. Use your hand to help you

out, but keep your mouth on his penis until you get the job completely done.

I would suggest practicing on a cucumber a few times before trying it out on your man, but keep in mind it's actually easier to perform this technique on a penis than a cucumber because the condom holds better.

Some important things to remember, though:

You should lovingly caress his penis with your hand while performing this technique. It makes it more intimate and exciting for the man.

If your partner isn't circumcised, push his foreskin back before putting the condom on him – this leaves room for the foreskin to move back and forth smoothly during sex without breaking the condom.

Only use water-based lubricants like KY-Liquid™, Astroglide™ or Probe™ to lube up the head of your man's penis when putting on his condom. Oil-based lubricants such as Vaseline™, baby oil, hand creams, or mineral oil will decrease the strength of a latex condom and increase the chance of it breaking.

Don't put lubricant on his entire penis, just the tip. Otherwise the condom might slip off during sex.

When putting condoms on with your mouth you might want to buy those without spermicide as they can not only be nauseating, but can also leave your lips and mouth numb.

And lastly, keep in mind that once you've performed this technique on a man you're likely going to be able to get him to do anything you ask, and have him anticipating things you might not ask. I really believe it was this trick that sent Romeo over the top, and turned him into a little lap dog. Now you see how I earned those emerald earrings.

III.   *Mastering Vaginal Intercourse*

Okay, I'm going to get very elementary here. The most important thing to remember about sex, of course, is that you have to be an active and passionate participant in the act.

Don't just lay there like a wet rag! Move those hips, girl. When he's on a down thrust you should be moving your pelvis up to meet him each and every time. His balls should not be hitting the bed! And if you've been doing the pelvic thrust exercise I told you about in Chapter Two, you'll be meeting him with an energy that will astound and delight him. But don't just go straight up and down . . . move your hips in a circular manner for added enjoyment – yours and his!

You should also be putting your Kegel Exercises, which you also learned in Chapter Two to good use. If you've been doing them on the regular your vagina will already be tighter, which will automatically increase your partner's pleasure, but I want you to also give him an extra treat!

Wait until the head of his penis is about half-way in and give it a quick but forceful squeeze hello. If you've been doing the exercises on a regular basis he'll feel it, and the look on his face will tell you just how much he does. Then when his shaft is fully in, give it another squeeze, and then squeeze his head again when he's withdrawing for another thrust. Try to keep this up during the whole session – squeeze his head when it's going in, squeeze his shaft when he's fully in, squeeze his head on it's way out. It takes a little practice to get the timing down pact, but once you do you'll have your man in constant ecstasy, and boasting to his friends that he's found a woman with an "educated pussy."

And now's no time to be a silent partner. Men love to hear a woman make a bit of noise. Some like the woman to whisper dirty little nothings in their ear, others want to hear the woman tell them how good he is, some men just like to hear the woman moan or even scream. (For dramatic effect I like to loudly moan, and then bite down on the edge of the pillow as if I didn't I would scream loud enough to wake up the neighborhood. That really makes a man feel like he's doing something!)

Yet another sex tip!
Your man's been gone for months, or even years, and he's expecting when he hits that kitty it's going to be tight as all hell.

But wait! You went on the creep while he was away!

Oooooh! Shame on you!

Hell, I'm not going to try and judge; I'm going to try and help. In fact, I *am* going to help Here's a little known secret, dear sistas!

Ever heard of alum? It's a fine white powder commonly used in food processing and pickling. It's what gives pickles that crisp, crunchy texture, and is also an ingredient in baking powder. You can find it in the spice section of most supermarkets, and most drugstores also carry it.

Mix two to three teaspoonfuls in water and douche no more than an hour before having sex. It will cause your vaginal tissues to swell, and slightly dry, so sex won't be as pleasurable for you as it will be for him. You'll be almost as tight as a virgin!

But Caution! Repeated use of alum douche can cause yeast infections.

Okay, now I'm going to talk to you about a sexual subject many of you have read about (especially those of you who are fans of Zane or E. Lynn Harris) and may even be curious about, but have been too timid, or too afraid, to try.

I'm going to talk to you about anal sex.

Now, not all men are into this, but many men have tried it at least once, or wanted to. And some men are really, really into it. And some women are, too. As the old saying goes . . . try it, you might like it!

IV. Mastering Anal Sex

The reason most women are afraid to try anal sex is because we hear it's painful. And guess what? It can be. Extremely!

There are two muscle rings called sphincters, which surround the anal opening. You can pretty much control the tenseness of the external sphincter at will, much the way you decide to flex or unflex your toes.

The internal sphincter, however, is much different. This muscle is controlled by the involuntary part of your nervous system; which controls your heartbeat, pulse, and stress response. The internal sphincter can respond to your fear and anxiety during anal sex and tighten up – hence the pain.

So the trick is to get both sphincters to relax. Easier said than done.

The first thing, and this is important, you should not engage in anal sex unless you want to, and are ready to. Otherwise, your body is going to respond to your reluctance, and make the whole experience pretty damn horrific.

But should you decide to try it, here's how you should go about it.

1. First of all, I would strongly suggest that you have a nice long drink of

wine. Or maybe two. Hell, maybe three. Get yourself feeling comfy, sexy, and relaxed.

2. Have a water-based lubricant around, such as KY-Jelly™, Astroglide™, or ForePlay™. Please, do remember that the lubricant has to be water-based, because as I said before oil-based lubricants such as Vaseline™, or hand lotions or creams will break down the latex in a condom and cause it to break or tear. Also, using an oil-based lubricant for anal sex can lead to bacterial infections later on.

3. Make sure you use condoms! Because anal tissue is so fragile it's most likely to sustain tiny tears, which may be painless, but will increase the possibility of the spread of the HIV-virus because the infection can easily invade your system through the tears. That's why HIV is much more easily transmitted during anal sex than vaginal sex.

4. And most importantly of all, have a partner that you trust will not get carried away with excitement and

disregard your instructions to stop or slow down should you desire them to do so.

5. When you see people engaging in anal sex in porno films, or read about them doing it in books, the most common position they use is Doggy-style. That's all fine and good for women who are used to anal sex, but I would recommend that beginners use the Side-by-Side position – with the woman facing away from the man. This allows the woman more control. And it is very important that the woman be in control, at least in the beginning.

6. You can't just jump into anal sex. You and your partner should engage in foreplay, a lot of kissing, hugging, nibbling and sucking, and you should be on the receiving end this time around, ladies. Your partner should be doing everything possible to get you feeling excited and uninhibited.

7. While engaging in the foreplay your partner should take his finger and rub the opening of your anus. Believe it or not, you'll probably find this quite

exciting because the anus opening is full of nerve endings that can give quite a bit of pleasure.

8. Now, try to consciously relax your sphincters and have your partner slowly insert a well-lubricated finger into your anus. (How much lubricant is enough? When you think you're using way too much lubricant, that's just the right amount. No kidding!) Your partner should be playing with your clit and nibbling your neck as he's doing this, to keep you in a receptive state of excitement.

9. Once you get used to the one finger, have him insert another over-lubricated finger inside your anus. He should push no further than you feel comfortable with. He should do a little wiggling of those two fingers while inside you. A little thrusting, but not much, but some nice little wiggling. When you're used to the feeling of having two fingers inside, you're ready to move on to bigger and better things!

10. Your partner should move his well lubricated condom-sheathed penis to

the opening of your anus, and slowly push in so that the head just barely penetrates the rim – there should be little or no pain at this point since he's not actually pushing inside.

11. It's now up to you! Instead of the man slowly pushing inside of you, you should now take control. Once you're comfortable with your anal hole being slightly open, at your leisure and comfort, you should slowly back up into him. Your partner should be playing with your clit, while nibbling your neck, and whispering all kinds of sweet nothings in your ear while you slowly push back toward him, and you should feel free to pause or stop whenever you feel the need.

12. Okay, now that he's fully in, he should take over, and he'll start thrusting in and out as if he were in your vagina, but he should be very considerate of your comfort level. Usually beginners don't enjoy the man coming all the way out and then pushing back all the way in. He should only come out about halfway before pushing his way back in. And

remember – if you want him to stop don't hesitate to tell him so.

So, there! You've done it! That wasn't so bad, was it? Like I said earlier, some women enjoy anal sex, and between you and me, I'm one of those women. No, I don't make it a regular part of my sexual regime, but I do love it as an occasional change of pace.

And yes, a woman can definitely reach orgasm while having anal sex!

But here's an important thing for you to know:

Never let a man withdraw from your rectum and then enter your vagina without changing his condom and washing! You can get lots of different vaginal infections if you do.

V.   Mastering Oral Sex

Unlike anal sex, Ladies, this one you have to do. Yeah, that's right, I said you have to do it, so stop frowning up!

I mean, come on, how many of you know men who don't love blowjobs? In all my years I've only met one, and I still can't figure out what the hell was wrong with him.

But the thing is if you approach it like it's something you have to do simply to please your man not only will you not enjoy it, he won't get the full enjoyment either because he'll sense your reluctance.

Ladies, think of it like this, you should *want* to give your man a blowjob if only because in doing so you're pleasing him, and when you really please him he's likely to want to find other ways to please you so that you'll keep pleasing him. Did that sound confusing? Just think about it for a minute and I'm sure you'll get it.

So not only should you want to give your man a blowjob, you should want to be good at it. And listen, once you master the art of giving good blowjobs you'll be so proud of how you make him feel you will actually enjoy giving them. Really!

So how do you give a good blowjob? It's not hard. (No pun intended.)

a. The two most common positions for performing fellatio is to have him lie down and you lean over him, or have him standing while you kneel in front of him. I find most men prefer you on your knees in front of them. No big wonder as to why, huh? It makes them feel like the woman is the subservient participant in this endeavor. (Another very common position is the 69, where one partner lays on top of the other, both giving the other oral sex. This can be fun, but not really conducive for being the best at your game since your movement is limited. I would recommend beginners stick to the first two positions mentioned.).

b. Hold his penis firmly, but gently with one hand near the middle of the shaft, while caressing the entire penis with the other. If you're in the kneeling position, this is the time you look up at him with your big (or small) beautiful eyes. Men love it when you look at them adoringly while you're touching their penis. It makes them feel that it's an object of admiration.

c. Smile, and then pucker your lips and kiss the tip of the head of his penis. Then take your tongue and flick it over the little slit. Close your eyes and go "mmm," like it's the best thing you've ever tasted. Look up at him again and smile.

d. Slowly flick your tongue around the head of his penis, paying especially close attention to the frenulum – this is the area on the underside of the penis, where head meets the shaft. It looks like the ligament on the underside of your tongue, which is also called a frenulum. This is THE most sensitive part of a man's penis!

e. While you're flicking your tongue over his head and frenulum, use your free hand (you still should have one hand holding his penis at the middle of the shaft) to *gently* caress and massage his testicles.

f. Still maintaining your tongue action, take your free hand and massage the area of skin between his scrotum and his anus. This area is known as the perineum, and is one of the most sensitive parts of a man's body. You can look up at your man to see his reaction, but chances are you won't have to, he'll probably be purring like a kitten.

g. Now, use your tongue to flicker around the head one more time, then go to the very tip and give a quick lick, then give it a gentle kiss.

h. Form your mouth into a perfect "O" shape, tucking your lips over your teeth, and take the head of his penis – and only the head – into your mouth and start a slight sucking action. Bat those beautiful eyes of yours at your man when you begin this step. He wants to know that you like what you're doing!

i. Take the hand that you've been using to hold his penis, and move it up the shaft so that it meets where your mouth is enclosed around his head. Shape your hand like it's a ring, and use it to enclose his penis. This adds length to your mouth, which you'll need since the average mouth is two to three inches and the average penis is five to six inches. (Yes, it's a sad truth . . . the eight inch dick is the exception!) The combination of your hand and mouth should give you a tunnel of about five inches to work with. It makes him feel like you're taking five inches of him inside your mouth when you may only be taking in two or three.

j. Using your mouth and your hand, move up and down the head and shaft of his penis, swirling your tongue around his penis as you go up and down. Remember to use your free hand to caress and massage his scrotum and perineum. And remember you should be the one moving, not him. That way you keep control so he doesn't thrust too far inside your mouth causing you to choke.

k. Go up and down the head and shaft of his penis for awhile, but then go back to steps d through f. Now this will give your jaws a needed respite, but also the alternation adds to the man's excitement.

l. You should also use your tongue and flick up and down the seam that runs along the underside of the penis.

m. Lick his scrotum, and you can even gently (men get paranoid when you handle this part of their anatomy) take them into your mouth.

n. Don't just massage the perineum with your hand; move your tongue down there and really give your man a thrill!

o. Go back to the up and down motion on the head and shaft.

Okay, so the important things to remember are the batting of the eyes, the flick around the frenulum, the caressing and massaging of the scrotum, the tunnel technique (placing your hand close to your mouth to increase depth), the swirling of the tongue, the tongue flick along the seam on the underside of the penis, and most important of all, act like you're enjoying yourself. Like there's nothing you'd rather be doing.

Now get ready to add some variety!

- Of course there's always the tried and true trick of putting a layer of whip cream and/or chocolate around his penis.
- Some men also like it when you alternate your mouth temperatures by putting crushed ice into your mouth before blowing him, or drinking a hot drink beforehand.
- Mints can also be exciting. Putting an Altoid™ or menthol mint in your mouth before

giving your man a blowjob can cause a tingling and numbness of your man's genitals.

- Humming can also be fun. It causes a vibrating sensation which some men find stimulating.

Caution – please be very, very careful to keep your teeth off your man's penis! And make sure your hands are perfectly manicured. You don't want a ragged nail to have your man howling in pain. Nothing can break the mood faster than a bleeding dick!

Oh, my God, I can't believe it! You're now an expert! You've now mastered the art of the blowjob! I'm so proud!

But, ahem, now there are other things we need to discuss.

Deep-Throat – Once upon a time there was a woman named Linda Lovelace. Now this chick was weird. She was so weird, even she thought she was weird. See, the thing is she couldn't have an orgasm unless some guy was shoving his johnson down her throat. She went to a doctor to find out why that was, and upon examining her he found that her clitoris was located in the back of her throat!

Sounds like bullshit? Well, that's because it is. But it was the premise of the best selling porno flick of all time, "Deep Throat." The plot was ridiculous, the acting was horrible, and the cinematography was laughable. And yet it grossed more than $600 million in sales.

Why? Because in half the film Linda Lovelace has a pair of balls slamming up against her lips, and that shit turns men on.

I hate Linda Lovelace; she made it hard for the rest of us (again, no pun intended.).

Yes, I do know how to Deep Throat, but I don't do it every time I go down on a man, and I don't do it throughout the act. I'll usually start Deep Throating right when I sense the man is about to cum, or I'll do it if he's taking to long too come and I have other things to do. How the hell Linda Lovelace could keep that shit up for twenty or thirty minutes at a time is simply beyond me.

Now, most women can Deep Throat, though most women think they can't. That's because we have a gag reflex that kicks in anytime any foreign object (such as a penis) comes near our tonsils and makes us feel as if we're going to vomit so we stop, thinking we just can't complete the act.

The trick is learning to control the gag reflex. You have to relax the muscles at the back of your throat, and the only way to do this is with practice. The good news is that these muscles seem to have a "memory." Once you're able to take a penis a certain depth into your throat you'll always be able to take in the same amount without gagging.

So the first thing to do is find someone to practice on. I wouldn't announce, though, that "Gee, I want to learn how to Deep Throat. Can I practice on you?" Instead, while you're performing fellatio on him, look up with those beautiful eyes, and say, "Baby, I want to feel you all the way deep inside my throat -- but I've never done it before so I want to go slow, okay?" Believe me, no man is going to turn you down simply because you're a trainee!

The thing to remember is you have to stay in control! If your partner starts ramming his johnson down your throat get off your knees and throw his ass out. Not only do you not want to practice with this guy, you don't want anyone that inconsiderate and uncaring in your life!

But once you have the man whom you feel comfortable practicing on, here's what you do.

    a.   The kneeling position is fine, as long as your head is lined up slightly below his groin area, so that you have to tip your chin up to take his penis into your mouth. That helps align your mouth and throat. If the kneeling position won't work for you, you might want to try lying on the bed on your back with your head hanging down over the edge.

b. Start performing fellatio on him, using the techniques mentioned earlier. When you're ready to start Deep Throating, take his head in your mouth and give it a quick twirl with your tongue. Then exhale, and press your tongue down against the palate of your mouth and open your throat as if the doctor was going to insert a tongue depressor or a cotton swab.

c. Push your head forward on his penis until you just begin to feel the gag reflex kick in, then pause – but do not make him withdraw from your mouth – wait a second or so, then try to open your throat wider and see if you can take him in a little farther. Tears may spring into your eyes here – but it's not due to pain. It's just a normal reaction when you're messing with your gag reflex.

    d. Pull your head back so that head of his penis is at the edge of your lips, and open your mouth – with him still inside – and take a deep breath and then exhale. Then repeat steps b and c.

    e. While Deep Throating, contract your throat muscles around his penis as if you were doing your Kegel Exercises.

It's going to take some time to get the hang of it, and don't think you're going to be able to fully Deep Throat him the first couple of times you try, but practice really does make perfect.

And I really, truly and honestly, do recommend every woman at least try to perfect the technique of Deep Throating. If you can't get with it, that's okay; at least you can say you tried and then just use the hand and mouth tunnel technique to make him happy.

If you do master it – so much the better. You get to feel such a sense of accomplishment when you can give a man a blowjob and have his balls slapping against your chin. And your man will be ever so grateful!

Okay. Now I have to talk to you about a subject many of you will find downright *distasteful*. Swallowing.

No! Don't close this book! Don't walk away! Just hear me out for a minute! Come on now . . . you've gone this far!

I know the thought of a man ejaculating in your mouth might be repulsive, and I'm not going to lie to you and say that once you try it you'll enjoy it (although some women do.). But I urge you to try it at least once, and then you can decide if you'll ever do it again.

I promise you, promise you, that once you swallow a man's cum it's something he'll never forget and will always be grateful for.

But I also promise that I won't hold it against you if you try it once and then never do it again. But the thing is once you see the reaction of your man, the lasting reaction of your man, you might realize it's in your benefit to keep this procedure in your little bag of tricks.

I know the first thing you have to get over is the actual thought of it, but swallowing a man's sperm is no more nasty or harmful than swallowing his saliva when you kiss.

If it's the taste you're worried about, well, I'm sure you've heard that the taste of a man's sperm depends on his diet. Men who drink hard liquor, smoke cigarettes or eat a lot of red meat tend to have a more bitter taste to their sperm. Don't read "more bitter" to mean "bad," it simply means more bitter. Men who eat a lot fruit and/or nuts, or drink a lot of fruit juice or wine tend to have a sweeter tasting sperm.

In addition, the consistency of sperm might turn a lot of women off. It has the texture of a light lotion, and therefore actually not easy to simply swallow. I'm not going to lie – it definitely leaves an aftertaste.

There are some women who will let the man ejaculate in their mouth and then go to the bathroom and spit it out. Personally, I think this is stupid. This way she tastes it going in, and also tastes it going out. Why not just swallow the wad and get it over with once and for all?

Also, and I can't explain the psychology behind this, but men seem to get upset when they know that a woman is spitting out their sperm. They seem to feel rejected on some level. I think it better not to let him cum in your mouth at all rather than spit it out.

I do have one friend who's slick enough to let a man ejaculate in her mouth and then trick him into thinking she's swallowing. While the man is cumming she's steady sucking, but at the same time pushing the sperm out the sides of her mouth. He may see it coming out, but thinks his wad is so huge that she can't swallow it all without some trickling out. Puleeze!

Do I swallow? Yep. Although not every single time, or with every single man I've been with. But you can bet your bottom dollar when I'm working on a man to get something out of him I'm giving him head, I'm Deep Throating, and I'm swallowing.

Which brings me to my own little personal tip. While I'm not repulsed by the taste of sperm I don't particularly like it either—so I only swallow if I'm using the Deep Throat technique. And then I make sure that when he ejaculates that his penis is deep enough down my throat that the sperm is past my taste buds, and simply slides down my throat. Very little aftertaste, if any, at all!

So we've pretty much covered oral sex here, right? Please don't think because I'm not talking about the man giving you oral sex (cunnilingus) I don't think it's essential for a man to reciprocate. That's not the case at all! Any man who is a good lover, or a considerate person, will go down on you as readily as you go down on him. But this book (and specifically this chapter) is about driving your man wild in bed.

Okay, now I won't make any more mention of oral sex, okay? At least not in this chapter.

Except to say, that if you simply can't bring your self to perform oral sex on your man (oh, you sexually uptight woman, you!) then you should at least make sure you give him good hand-jobs. And even if you do give him oral sex you should still learn how to give a good hand-job.

VI.   Mastering The Hand-Job

The key to giving a good hand-job is to have plenty of lubricant at hand (Okay, pun intended!). It doesn't matter if the lubricant is oil or water-based because you're going to wash it off before putting on a condom to have sex, otherwise the condom might slip off in your vagina. You might even want to use some of the flavored lubricants, just in case you go from hand-job to blowjob.

This is also a good time to remind you that your hands should be in good shape, well manicured and looking good.

First let me admit that when I first started giving hand-jobs all I was doing was basically jerking the guy off. I actually learned how to do a real hand-job by a man who was tired of me just pulling on his penis.

So now I'll instruct you.

Now for the steps!

a. Pour a generous amount of lubricant in the palm of your hands and then rub them together to warm up the lubricant.

b. Place one hand around the base of his shaft so that the back of your hand is facing you and your thumb is pressed against his pubic hair.

c. Move your hand up the shaft to the head of his penis in one single continuous motion.

d. When you get to the head of his penis, twist your hand slightly as if you were opening a jar.

e. Without removing your hand from his penis, move your palm to the very top of the head, then with an open palm rub and rotate your hand over it

f. As you're doing this, put your other hand in the starting place of your first.

g. Now bring your first hand down over the head again, and – this time with your thumb facing you and your four fingers facing his stomach – bring your hand down in one single continuous motion so that it rests on top of your second hand.

h. Remove the first hand and bring your second hand up in the same manner as you did the first, making sure you do the twist when you get to the head and rotate and rub when you get to the tip.

i. Continue to alternate hands until your man reaches his climax.

Well now ladies, now you know how to give a very electrifying hand-job. Make sure you give yourself a hand . . . but only after you given your man one!

Okay, I realize you all know all the positions, but just in case, let's go over them one time real quick, okay?

Really there are only five or six main sexual positions, though there are a bunch of variations on each. Personally, I believe variety is the spice of life, so be sure to be adventurous. You'll have to experiment to find out which position is your favorite, but be sure to try them all. I'm sure you'll find there's a time and place where one might be more appropriate than the other.

1. Missionary Position

This is the traditional position for sex, at least in the Western world – the man on top and the woman on the bottom. But don't read traditional as dull or boring; this is one of the most intimate sexual positions. It allows for a lot of kissing, caressing and whispering.

The missionary position is also conducive to easy entry, but to maximize penetration (especially if the woman is heavy set or the man has a small penis) you should place pillows under your butt. A word of caution here, while decorative pillows look and feel nice under your butt, it's quite likely they're going to smell like sex afterward, and even perhaps have semen stains. It's best to use your everyday pillows with standard pillowcases that you can throw in the laundry afterward.

Another way to ensure better penetration is to wrap your legs around his hips. Men usually find this quite exciting because it makes them feel you're saying you can't get enough of them.

To *truly* maximize penetration, and impress him with your sexual astuteness, you should try placing your legs on his shoulders. A word of caution here, if the man is overly endowed giving him that much access can be a bit painful.

And another word of caution the two above variations will almost always result in the man reaching his orgasm quickly, so if you want your man to last awhile, you might want to save these positions for the last on your list during your lovemaking session.

There are drawbacks to the missionary position, however; if the man is overweight it can be uncomfortable for the woman and even make it difficult for her to breathe at times.

Also, while your clitoris will receive some stimulation from his pubic area meeting yours, it's not conducive for manual clitoral stimulation. This can be extremely problematic because many women can only experience orgasm if their clits are actively stimulated – either by their partner or themselves.

2. Doggy-Style

This is a position that brings out the animal in most men, and is also one of the most pleasurable for most women. For the position the woman is on all fours, and the man kneels behind her and enters her vagina from the back.

Doggy-style allows a man to fully penetrate a woman, and watch himself while doing so – a real turn-on for a man. You do know that men are much more visually stimulated than woman, right? That's why they like to masturbate with open girlie magazines – but when you're doing it doggy-style *you're* the girlie, girlie! Since his hands are free during Doggy-style this also allows him to play with his testicles during sex, and gives you the opportunity to play with his balls, too.

The reason women love Doggy-style is because it gives the man the most direct access to their G-Spot. (Ooh-la-la!) It also makes it easy for a man to reach down and play with your clitoris, or for you to play with your own.

Everyone benefits!

In addition, since both partners have a wide range of movement in this position the man and woman can take turns being in control. Either the woman can be the relatively passive partner (you still have to do your vaginal squeezes and hip movements!) and allow the man to do the thrusting, or he can be still and allow the woman to push back and forwards on his shaft at her will.

However, Doggy-style can be very painful if your man has a large penis, because men love to slam themselves into you when in this position and they can actually hit your uterus or cervix. Ouch!

Doggy-style has many variations, and to be truthful, I enjoy each and every one.

One variation is for the woman to lie on her stomach with the man on top. This allows the woman to close her legs, thereby causing more friction for the man, but also limiting his penetration.

Another variation is for you to have your arms and chest flat on the bed while your butt is in the air, this gives him an opportunity for deeper penetration.

Still another variation is for the woman to be standing on the floor bending over and holding onto a chair or table (or bathroom sink!) while the man penetrates her from behind. I've found that most men prefer this position, so make sure you hurry and get your rocks off because it won't be long before he gets his!

3. Woman on Top Position

Ride 'em Cowgirl! Yee-Hah! This is the position that gives YOU the most control and feeling of domination, and allows the man to just lay back and enjoy.

Quite simply, the man lies on his back and the woman straddles him, taking his penis into her vagina. While sitting astride him she can move her hips in either a thrusting or rocking motion. The up and down thrusts are more stimulating for the man, but they should be broken up with some rocking back and forth.

I like this position because it allows me to "tease" my partner. I like going up and down for a few minutes, then pulling almost all the way up so that the tip of his penis is just barely inside of me. While hovering over him in that manner I'll say something like, "Do you like it?" or "Do you want it?" or "Tell me how much you want it." Believe me, you can get a man to say or agree to just about anything when you have him in this position!

Another benefit of The Woman On Top position is that it gives both you and your partner full access to your breasts and clitoris during the lovemaking, so one or both of you should be playing away to your heart's contentment.

For a fun change of pace, have your partner open his legs slightly, and then lie down flat on him while he's still inside you so that you're in the position that he's usually in when you're doing it missionary style. Now, tightly close your legs and start thrusting up and down so that your thighs are squeezing his penis as you go up and down on it. Guaranteed to drive your man crazy!

Another variation is known as the Reverse Cowgirl. In this position the man lies on his back and the woman once again straddles him, but with her back toward him. The woman can hold the man's knees for leverage as she moves up and down on the man's penis.

And yet another variation is known as the Romantic Embrace. The woman sits on top of the man – with his penis inside her – and her legs pointed straight out. The man then sits up and the two embrace. Don't move – just sit there looking in each other's eyes, kissing, and talking softly. I wouldn't recommend this position for just any couple, but if the man and woman are in love this pose can be very sensuous and erotic.

4. Side-by Side Position

The Side-by-Side positions are great for slow, lazy type lovemaking. In fact, these positions are great when you're all tuckered out from sex and want to have just plain old lazy sex, and perhaps fall asleep afterward with your partner inside you.

For Side-to-Side position with the partners facing each other, the man and woman can start in the Missionary Position and then simply roll over to their side – the man's legs would be between the woman's. Because his hips are somewhat restricted, his thrusts won't be as deep as in other positions, nor as rapid. This is an extremely romantic position because the couple can gaze into each other's eyes while they slowly make love.

Probably the most common variation of the Side-by-Side position is known as spooning. That's when the man and woman are laying down side-by-side with the man facing the woman's back. The man generally slings one arm over the woman's hips to draw her close to him, making this an extra intimate position since it's one in which the woman feels secure and protected.

5. Standing Up Positions

If you've never tried it standing up just go ahead and close this book, because you don't have an adventurous bone in your body.

Having sex while standing up isn't the most romantic, or the best position for deep penetration, or the most comfortable, but damn if it isn't the most exciting! You don't need to take off all of your clothes, and you can do it in a cramped space (like a broom closet or airplane bathroom). Makes you feel downright naughty!

Standing Up positions are easiest when both partners are about the same height, but a greater disparity in heights shouldn't be a deterrent, and in fact can be fun.

The two of you should start off facing each other in a loose embrace with your legs open and his in between yours. The man should then bend his knees so that his penis is at the entrance of your vagina, then stand back up – entering you as he does so.

If the man is a lot taller, and stronger, when he starts thrusting he can actually pick you up off your feet. Now, that's fun! Wrap your legs around his waist and let him go at it!

If he's not all that strong, you can brace your back against the wall to help him out with support.

For variety, have your back toward him while you brace your hands against the wall and bend slightly at the waist while he enters you from behind.

<u>How To Drive Him Wild In Bed – Part II</u>

Okay, we've already talked about the more traditional methods of sex, but I think it's time for us to talk about some of the more untraditional methods.

Okay?

Okay?

Okay?

Some of the things you might already indulge in with your partner, and others you might find downright nasty and decide right off you're never going to do . . . but do at least try to keep an open mind, okay?

For instance do you know that most men love to have a woman rub a finger over his anus while she's blowing him? It's not so strange if you think about it because, as I mentioned before, there are a lot of sensitive nerve endings located at the opening of the anus.

And some men, quite a few men, like it when a woman inserts her finger in his anus while she's blowing him or they're having sex. Not all men, but many men. If you're rubbing his anal opening and he starts thrusting his ass upwards, he's trying to give you a hint. Take it.

Did you know that men have a G-spot also? While a woman's G-spot is located inside her vagina, a man's is inside his anus. We know it as the prostrate.

To find it, insert your well-lubricated index finger (do I have to remind you to only use water-based lubricants?) into your partner's anus up to the second knuckle. Press your finger back in a "come-hither" motion, and you should be able to feel the prostrate through the front part of the rectal wall. It's about the size of a pigeon's egg. Massage it for a moment. This will send many men through the roof, and cause an intense orgasm.

We also need to talk about Tossing Salads. No . . . it has nothing to do with lettuce and tomatoes. The phrase is used as a euphemism for analingus, or oral sex performed on someone's anus.

Oooh, girl . . . look at you frowning up your face! Stop it now! You're only hastening the onset of wrinkles!

I've never met a man who *expects* his partner to toss his salad, but I've met very few men who didn't enjoy it, either. Whether you do it or not is totally up to you, I make no judgments.

But I would be derelict if I didn't tell you that there are diseases that can be contracted through analingus. Chief among these are Hepatitis A or E. coli, though the risk of contracting HIV is low.

The key, though, to anal play is cleanliness. If you know you and your man are going to be engaging in anal play I would suggest that you take a bath or shower together, and make sure that you clean your anal areas well. Also, consider using a barrier such as a piece of plastic wrap or a latex dental dam if you're going to be Tossing Salads. .

Let me also take this opportunity to say that just because a man likes limited anal play doesn't mean that's he's on the downlow or is in the least bit interested in homosexuality. You have to keep in mind that women don't have a

131

prostrate gland, and therefore we can not even begin to understand the pleasure a man can feel having a woman insert a finger, or even a sex toy inside his rectum. But while they may crave the feeling of a well lubricated finger massaging their prostrate it doesn't mean that they want a man to insert his penis in him, or that he wants to insert his penis into another man. By the way, we're going to discuss bisexual men in a later chapter, okay?

And then there are a lot of men who want to experiment with new things, but don't know how to bring it up to a woman. They might not even know they want to experiment.

I was dealing with one man, an electrical engineer, who was one of the most sexually conservative men I've ever met. The poor guy, who was a card-carrying Republican, was only interested in the Missionary Position, and would only do it with the lights off. But something told me there a wild man ready to be unleashed.

One day I went over to his apartment with a small black velvet drawstring duffel bag that I carelessly threw onto an armchair. When he asked me what was in it, I said, "Would you believe that one of the girls at work invited me to one of those sexy lingerie party, and I won some kind of door prize. She said it's a goody-bag or something, but I didn't bother to look in it because I was late getting over here. I don't even know what's inside."

He shrugged, and I left it at that until he had a couple of martinis. Then I put on some music and started doing a few sensuous dance moves in front of him as I slowly sipped on my own martini. I went over and kissed him on the neck and nibbled his ear, but when he reached to pull me in his arms I backed away laughing and innocently fell back into the armchair where I had thrown the good-bag.

"Oh, that's right," I said with a little giggle, "I forgot all about this. Let's see what's in here."

I made us a couple of more drinks then moved back over to the couch where he was sitting and sat next to him with the bag in my lap. I took off my shoes and started massaging his leg with my foot as I began to pull items out of the bag. The first was a black silk blindfold.

"Oh, look at this," I said with a chuckle. "Ooh, maybe I should have you blindfold me so you can have your way with me, huh?" He kind of nodded, with a little smile on his face. Then I said, "Or maybe I should blindfold you and do all kinds of nasty things to you, huh?" He smiled again, but I noticed his eyes momentarily lit up.

"Now what can this be for?" I asked as I pulled a string of black pearls from the goody-bag.

He picked up the pearls and fingered them. "I have no idea," he said finally.

"Ooh, I know. I remember reading about these in a book. I think they're called love pearls. I think you put them in your butt."

"You do what?" he asked.

"You put them in your butt and then your partner pulls them out slowly one pearl at a time, I answered. "It's supposed to be very exciting. I've always wanted to see what they looked like."

I then pulled out an erection ring. "Now see this I've seen before," I said while taking a sip of my drink.

"What is it?" he said, taking it in his fingers and twirling it around.

"An erection ring." I answered. "You put it on near the base of your erect penis before you have sex. It stops you from ejaculating too quickly and also increases your sensitivity. At least that what's I've heard and read."

"Is that right?" he said examining the ring even more closely now.

"Will you look at this?" I said pulling out a thin rubber five-inch dildo, powered by a removable vibrating bullet. "This thing is so thin I wouldn't think a woman would get more pleasure from it. Look, it's no wider than my finger."

"And what do we have here?" I asked, pulling out a small bottle labeled 'Warming Liquid.' I poured a small amount on my wrist and blew on it. "Oh, now that feels good." I then put a small amount on the back of his hand and blew. "See, "I said as his eyes widened. "It gets warm when you blow on it." I winked at him and then poured some more lotion in my hand while I unbuttoned his shirt with the other. I rubbed the lotion on his nipples and then began nibbling and blowing on them.

"Why don't we move this into the bedroom," he said in a breathless tone. "And bring the bag with you so we can see what else is in there."

Fifteen minutes later he was blindfolded and tied to the bedposts while I slowly dripped hot wax onto his bare back as he moaned and groaned in delight.

By the end of the week we had tried every item in the bag (including that thin 5-inch vibrating dildo which he soon found out was ideal for massaging his G-spot.) and had even gone down to a sex shop and bought more.

Not only had I turned him out, I turned him out so much I had to drop him. The man was wearing me out. Talk about unleashing a wild man!

And of course some men have their own little . . . um . . . sexual idiosyncrasies. It's up to you as to whether they're things you can deal with.

For instance some men like to go down on you after they've ejaculated inside your vagina.

Other men like a little water play. Meaning they might want to watch you urinate, or even have you pee on them.

And others, well, you get the idea. But what's important to remember is that nothing is abnormal or nasty unless it's abnormal or nasty to you.

Be always keep in mind that no one should try and force you to do anything you don't want to do. You are in charge of your own body and sexuality.

Okay, there's only one other thing that I do want to warn you about.

Videotaping. Sounds like fun, and it can be exciting to later watch yourself in action, but remember what happened to Paris Hilton and Pam Anderson. You never know when you're going to run into an unscrupulous partner who'll want to use the tapes against you.

How To Drive Him Wild Out Of Bed

"I want you to know you've ruined my life."

I looked up from the rum and coke I'd been nursing to see a former co-worker glaring at me. I glanced at my watch to see if I had enough time to bother asking her what horrible thing I'd done to her, and saw that I had a good twenty-five minutes before my train left Union Station for Boston where I was going to spend the weekend. Since I was at a bar at Union Station, and it would only take five minutes to walk to the tracks I decided to indulge the woman.

"It's good to see you, too," I said lightly as I motioned her to take a seat. "How's your mother?"

"She's fine," the ruined woman snapped as she unceremoniously plopped in the chair. "But I want you to know that I followed your advice and you've ruined my life."

"Uh-huh, you've already told me that" I said as I took another sip of my drink. "Care to explain?"

"I met this really cute guy at a party a couple of months ago and I followed all of your tips on flirting, and he came home with me that night. Then I did everything you told me about how to impress a man in bed, I did the deep throat thing, the lifesaver thing, and even the putting the condom on for him with my mouth. He loved that, by the way."

"All men do," I said with a nod "But I gather he didn't call you the next day?"

"Oh, he called me the next day. In fact, he came over the next night. And then again two nights after that. And he called me at least twice a week for the two months." She said with a grimace.

"Okay?" I said slowly. "So what's the problem?"

"The problem was he'd call and ask if he could come over, and as soon as he got there he wanted a roll in the hay." She leaned over the table so that her face was only a few inches from mind. "And that's all he wanted. Just to get his rocks off and then he was out of there. Never even spent the night."

I made a face. "That's not good. I hope you dropped his ass."

"Of course I did," she said leaning back in her chair and giving a wave of the hand. "So then I meet this other great guy at a club about a month ago. I figured that I made the mistake of going to bed with the first dude too fast, so I made this guy wait almost two weeks before I gave up the goodies. But damn if I'm not in the same pattern. At least this guy does take me out to dinner and drinks before coming up to my place and having me fuck his brains out, but it's pretty much the same damn thing. He calls, we go out, go back to my place and then we screw, and then I don't hear from him again until he's horny, I guess."

I glanced at my watch again. I still had almost twenty minutes to go. "Okay, so how am I responsible for ruining your life?" I asked.

"Well, I came to you because I wanted advice on how to get a man, but now, thanks to you, all I can get are men who want to screw me to death. That's worse than not being able to get a man at all." She almost shouted.

"Girl, you'd better check yourself," I said in a low but stern voice. "It's not my fault if you've turned yourself into a booty call."

She put her hand on her hip. "What did you just call me?" she said with the classic head bob.

"I said, you'd better check yourself. Don't be making a scene up in here because I swear I'll walk away and let you have the stage to yourself," I told her in a warning voice.

She thought about it for a minute, then said in a softer voice," Well, I don't appreciate being labeled a booty-call."

"I'm not the one who labeled you," I said with a shrug. I'm just the one who told you that you've been labeled."

"Well, how did that happen? Are you saying that every woman who's good in bed is going to be considered a booty-call?"

"Only the lop-sided ones," I answered.

"The what ones?"

"The women who spend their time perfecting their performance in bed, but don't worry about their performance out of bed."

"What do you mean?"

"Just what I said." I started gathering my things. I still had a good ten minutes before I needed to leave to catch the train, but I had decided I wasn't going to waste any more time on the silly heifer. I should never have given her the benefit of my wisdom in the first place.

"Wait," she said putting her hand on my elbow to delay my departure. "So are you going to tell me what I should do to turn this around?"

I pulled away, and slipped the strap of my overnight bag over my shoulder. "Well, considering how grateful you seem for my prior advice, the answer to that question would be no."

I then haughtily walked away.

The woman was right; of course, I had made a mistake in giving her the partial benefit of my advice without filling her on all she needed to know. And if she had approached me in even a halfway decent manner I would have rectified my error. But since she came at me in such a bitchy manner, to hell with her. She needed to figure it out on her own. But I refuse to let you – my dear readers who shelled out fifteen dollars for my little book – make the same mistake she did. I don't want anymore damn lop-sided disciples.

I've said it before but it bears repeating, a Sensuous Black Woman has a good attitude – about herself and the world around her. A pleasant attitude. Learn how to compliment people, but use sincere compliments. Be a good listener. Smile at people. Simply put, just be nice, okay? And if you find that by and large you just don't like people and find it hard to be pleasant, you need to see a counselor or do some kind of self-meditation, because the problem lies within you, not the people around you.

Okay, moving right along . . .

You should know that no matter how good you are in bed, you should be making the man feel that it's really him who is the master in the bedroom. Make him think that he brings out the best in you. Have him believing he's the best lover in the world, and he simply brings out the best in you. Feed into that great big ego that all men have.

Another thing you should know is that you need to make a man feel as good out of bed as you make him feel in bed.

This is essential!

Make him feel smart.

Make him feel handsome.

Make him feel irresistible.

Make him feel he's the only man in the universe.

Everybody – man, woman, or child – wants to believe that they are special. It's up to you to make the man that you've set your sights on feels so.

1. <u>Make him feel smart</u>.

One way to accomplish this is find out what's he's passionate about and then talk to him about it, and ask him questions about it. But ask intelligent questions. You should never let a man believe that you're a dummy. You'll be treated accordingly.

If he's a stock broker, tell him you've always been amazed at Wall Street moguls like Warren Buffett, and how they have the uncanny ability to know just when to buy into a company stock and when to sell. Then ask him how Martha Stewart actually got convicted for insider-trading. Then sit back and let him spout off his wisdom, making sure you nod whenever appropriate and be so appreciative of his knowledge. Of course this won't work if you don't know who Warren Buffett is or that Martha did a stint for insider-trading.

If he's a professional basketball player make sure you know where his team is in the standings, and the names of players on other teams who play the same position as him.

If he's a movie producer tell him you love movies, but always wondered how someone became a producer.

If he's a rap artist tell him you've heard real horror stories about what artists go through trying to make it into the industry and are the stories really true.

You've GOT to be well-read, so that even if you don't know a lot about his passion or profession, you know a little something-something, and give him that something-something and ask him for more.

That's what the Geishas and French courtesans I mentioned in Chapter One were so especially good at. They made sure they kept on top of what was going on in the world so they could converse intelligently with their chosen male partners, and with their male partner's friends.

Read at least one newspaper a day. Make it a point to watch television news programs once or twice a week. Keep up with what's going in politics. And read the gossip columns to get the skinny on what's going in the movie and music industries.

And don't worry about the fact that you might be more intelligent than your chosen, just don't lord it over him. Remember that a man's ego is fragile – while he might be impressed by your intelligence he never wants to feel like you're looking down on him because of his lack thereof.

2. <u>Make him feel handsome.</u>

Don't gush too much over a man's looks because men catch a case of the big head much faster than women, but do pick out one or two physical traits and compliment him on it. Even the homeliest of men have something going for them. Maybe it's their eyes. Or the broadness of their chest. Or their strong hands. Or their lop-sided smile. Whatever it is, make sure he catches you looking at it from time-to-time, and then lower your eyes and laugh and tell him you're really attracted to whatever it is he caught you looking at.

Just like a woman can't resist a man who makes her beautiful, a man can't resist a woman who makes him feel handsome. Especially if he's not!

3.   Make him feel irresistible.

Sexually that is. Initiate sex and sex games outside of the bedroom, and especially out of the house.

- If the two of you are out to dinner with friend, slip off your shoe and rub your foot against his leg while having a conversation with other people at the table. Better yet, if the two of you are sitting next to each other, reach under the tablecloth and start massaging his crotch while talking with the other people at the table. If the two of you are dining alone, do this while the waiter is taking his dinner order.

- When you and your man are talking while out in public, occasionally reach over and unobtrusively touch him on the shoulder or hand for absolutely no reason.

- Corner him when you're in an elevator alone, then whisper in his ear (even though you're alone, whisper, because whispering is just plain sensual) that you don't have on any panties, then move his hand under your dress as proof. Maybe he'll hit the emergency stop button and then lean you against the elevator wall and have at it, and maybe he won't. But you'd best believe he'll be thinking about it and with a huge hard-on to boot!

- Initiate sexual role-play in a public place. One of the best examples of this is in a book entitled "I'm Telling," by Karen E. Quinones Miller (In the spirit of full disclosure, Karen is a personal friend of mine and the publisher of this book, but I swear I would give this as an example even were this not the case.).

The heroine of the book goes into the bar and spots her boyfriend sitting with a couple of other men. She pretends she doesn't know him, but sends him a drink and makes a big deal of picking him up for a one-night stand. The other men were left dumbfounded and envious, and the boyfriend feels like he's the luckiest man alive.

- Call him up at his place of business and tell him you were just thinking about him. Tell him you were remembering your last lovemaking session and you started to get all hot and that your panties are now soaking wet. Then ask him to meet you for drinks after work.

- Stop by his office or apartment during your lunch break for some afternoon delight. If you have an hour or more, go ahead and have a full lovemaking session, but if you only have fifteen minutes to a half-hour settle for a quickie.

- Wearing a business suit, find some kind of excuse to get your partner down to the red-light district in your city, or a nearby town. While passing by a peepshow, make a big deal that you've never been to one and ask if he'll take you inside. Once in the booth, pretend to get hot while watching the show, the pull up the skirt of your business suit to reveal that you're not wearing panties.

- Have him take you to an R-rated movie, but make sure you find seats alone (you have a better chance of this if you go to an afternoon showing). When a love-making scene appears on film, start rubbing him through his pants. Believe me, he'll be taking you to a lot more movies!

- Call him and tell him you want to do something a little different tonight, then bring a porno film over.

- If he's into watching sports, learn the game but never be more expert than him. Pick a particular player on his favorite team, and then learn everything you can about him. Make comments about the player during the game, and cheer especially hard when that player makes a touchdown, homerun or three-point shot. But whatever you do, don't ask dumb questions when the game is on. Men don't find it cute at all, though they do love sharing their expertise with women who already have some knowledge about the sport.

- You like to be romanced? Men do, too, believe it or not. Do something surprising, and send him flowers at work (but only if he's already spent money on you!) with a nice card saying something like "Just because I was thinking of you," and sign it with your initials rather than your name. It will be the talk of the office and your man will be the center of attention.

4. <u>Make him feel he's the only man in the universe.</u>

- When you're out with your man make sure you're friendly and pleasant to the people around you, and especially his friends, but don't let anyone else nab your attention for long. If someone engages you in conversation, wait a few minutes then try and draw your man into the discussion.

- If you're engaged in a conversation across the room from your man, look over in his direction from time-time and flash him a smile, and even better, a wink. And flirt with him from across the room! Use the same techniques that used to hook him in the first place. They never grow old.

- I wouldn't advocate lying, but if a man is special to you, I don't see any reason why you shouldn't let him know. Tell him that you think he's wonderful and you're glad the two of you met.

The key thing is you have to show him that you're just as interesting, and as much fun, outside of the bedroom as you are inside. It's up to you to make him crave your company in public as well as in private.

<u>Picking The Right Man</u>

Oh Jerrod was just gorgeous.

He was about 5-foot-nine with a chestnut colored skin, and dreamy bedroom eyes.

He was articulate, had a master's degree in business administration, and was vice-president of Human Resources at a Fortune 500 company. Brother man was making real good money, and he didn't have a problem spending it on himself or on me.

And while he wasn't the most well-endowed man, Jerrod knew just what to do with the five inches that God had given him. I had absolutely no complaints about him in bed.

Jerrod was the perfect man. But as much as I wanted him to be, Jerrod just wasn't the perfect man for me.

He was the dullest person I'd met in my life.

It wasn't that he only wanted to stay home in the evenings, which he did; nor that he hated traveling for vacation, which he did. It was mainly that the man didn't know how to talk about anything but his job and his hobby, stamp collecting.

I was able to hang with him for about six months, but after that I introduced him to one of my friends who is a supervisor at the U. S. Post Office, and I wished them both the best of luck. I knew that Jerrod really wanted a monogamous relationship, but if I had stayed with him any longer I would have been cheating on him left and right just for some excitement. And while I have absolutely no problem going out with two, three, or four men at a time, when I'm in a serious relationship I don't cheat.

But while Jerrod wasn't the perfect man for me, he and my friend have now been happily married for two years. It just goes to show you that one woman's reject is another woman's treasure.

Be generous, if he's a good man but not for you pass him along to a friend with your blessing.

Most women are in search of her idea of the perfect man. For some women it's men with money. For others it has to be a man who looks like a movie star. Other women simply want a man who can offer her security. Still others want men with a little (or a lot) of thug in them. All women, though, want a man who will treat them well.

I have to admit that I'm into the material life so I look for generous men with cash. Could I love a man who didn't have a lot of money? Maybe. Probably. I guess so. And yet I'm not trying to find out. My grandfather used to tell me "Don't marry for money, marry for love. But go to where there's money and then fall in love." My gramps was one wise old man.

But obviously money isn't everything, or else I would still be with Jerrod. I make my own money – and while I like gifts and nice things, I don't have to depend on any man.

And ladies, if you're looking for a man with money, please don't limit yourself to athletes and music artists. Yes, they have a lot of money but the lifestyle they live isn't really conducive to having a healthy relationship. Women are constantly throwing themselves at these guys all the time, so it's hard for even the most determined of these men to stay faithful for any long period of time.

However, if you don't care about having a healthy relationship, and are just in it for the money and glam, then have at it. Have you ever stopped to consider though, that top-notch sports agents make just as much money as top-notch athletes? Think about it. An agent gets 15 percent of a player's salary, and chances are the agent has more than seven clients, don't you think? Do yourself a favor and do the math.

The same goes for the music industry. Performers make lots of money, but so do their agents and managers.

And of course there's lawyers, doctors, movie producers, stock brokers, and a host of other men who can rightfully boast they're in the high income bracket.

But please, my sistas, don't sell your soul for someone else's paycheck. Don't you *ever* let a man beat you down – physically or emotionally—just because he's worth six or seven figures.

My mother always said a man who makes $20,000 and brings you home half his paycheck is a better man than the one who makes $200,000 and gives you $20,000. Think about it. Don't diss a man simply because he makes a living working with his hands or drives a Hyundai instead of a Lexus. In the long run, a man's character means a lot more than his salary.

Crossing Racial Lines

Personally, I don't have a problem with Black women who date white men, or Black men who date white women – variety is the spice of life, and I think that love should be colorblind. But I do believe that Blacks who date exclusively outside of their race have issues that they need to address.

Bi-sexual Men

Many women won't knowingly date a switch-hitter, but if you make sure that he ALWAYS wears a condom when he's with you, there's really not much chance of catching any diseases, if that's your fear.

However, if you find out that your man has been hitting it off with other men and didn't tell you about it, you need to get rid of his ass. Not only is he sneaky and dishonest, but he might be putting your health at risk since you might sometimes get lax on the condom rule.

I don't play that downlow crap.

Finally, remember, a Sensuous Black Woman doesn't play a man, anymore than she would allow a man to play her. If you don't love him, don't tell him you do. That doesn't

mean you have to leave him alone, though. Just
don't ever promise more than you can deliver. It
can come back to bite you in the ass.

And So You're A Sensuous Black Woman

Congratulations!

Now that you've finished reading my little book and followed all of the guidelines, instructions, and advice you have all of the resources you need to become a Sensuous Black Woman.

I now just want to give you a very short lecture on responsibility.

A Sensuous Black Woman would never stomp on someone's feelings in order to get what she wants – especially another woman's feelings. If the man you want is dealing with your friend or relative, leave him the hell alone. He's off limits.

If the man you want is married and has children, why the hell do you want him? If he'll leave a wife and children for you then chances are he'll leave you for the next best thing that comes along. Don't play yourself like that.

If you're only interested in a man for a fling, don't lead him to believe that you want to start a real relationship with him. Don't play with other people's feelings.

And most importantly, be true to yourself. There is no one in the world who should be more important to you than you. There is no one in the world whom you should love more than you love yourself.

And keep this book around, we all need refresher courses from time-to-time.

Now go on out in the world and enjoy yourself as you show everyone what a Sensuous Black Woman can do.

I hope to see you out there!!!!!!!!!!!!!!!!

They're Back!

Essence® bestselling author Daaimah S. Poole revisits the unforgettable characters she created in *Got A Man*.

Ever since Shonda stole Malik from his fianceé—at the altar, no less—she's believed that marrying him would be her ticket to happiness. But when he finally steps up and makes it happen, Shonda is in for a rude awakening!

AVAILABLE FROM DAFINA BOOKS – MAY 2006
www.dspbooks.com

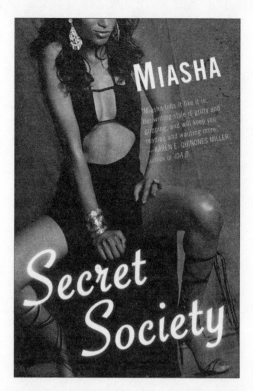

MIASHA

Miasha tells it like it is. Her writing style is gritty and gripping, and will keep you reading and waiting for more.
—KAREN E. QUINONES MILLER, author of IDA B.

Secret Society

"I WAS ON CLOUD NINE. NOTHING MADE ME HAPPIER THAN GREAT SEX AND MONEY AND THAT'S WHAT JAMES WAS GOOD FOR, BUT D*** IT IF I DIDN'T NEED MORE."
-CELESS

"CELESS, WHAT'S UP WITH YOU? I HEARD SOME WILD STUFF ABOUT YOU. YOU NEED TO CALL ME AS SOON AS POSSIBLE BECAUSE IF WHAT I FOUND OUT IS TRUE YOU'RE GOIN' TO HAVE SOME SERIOUS PROBLEMS."
-JAMES

"MY IMMEDIATE THOUGHT WAS THAT JAMES HAD FOUND OUT ABOUT O OR TARIQ OR BOTH. I NEVER EXPECTED IT TO BE THAT HE FOUND OUT I…"
-CELESS

"GIRL, WIPE YOUR EYES. DON'T BE CRYING OVER NO MAN. S***, JAMES WAS THE BROKEST OF THE THREE ANYWAY."
-TINA

"YOU KNOW WHAT B****, YOU F***ED WITH THE WRONG ONE!" POP! POP!
-SECRET SOCIETY

AVAILABLE FROM SIMON & SCHUSTER APRIL 2006
PREORDER NOW
WWW.MIASHA.COM

What's Done in the Dark
by
Gloria Mallette

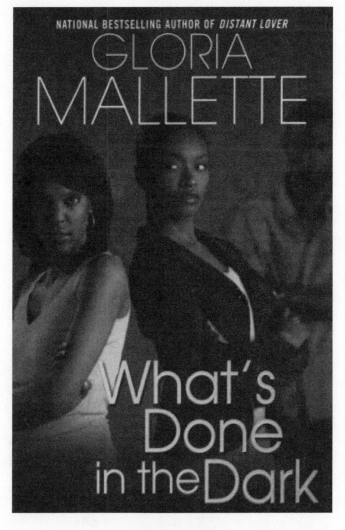

January, 2006
ISBN 0-7582-1157-0
Kensington Publishing
WWW.GLORIAMALLETTE.COM